I0796827

Surviving an Unwanted Divorce

A BIBLICAL, PRACTICAL GUIDE TO LETTING GO WHILE HOLDING YOURSELF TOGETHER

LYSA TERKEURST

WITH DR. JOEL MUDDAMALLE, JIM CRESS, AND SHAE HILL

An Imprint of Thomas Nelson

Surviving an Unwanted Divorce

Published by Nelson Books, an imprint of Thomas Nelson, 501 Nelson Place, Nashville, TN 37214, USA. Nelson Books and Thomas Nelson are registered trademarks of HarperCollins Christian Publishing, Inc.

Thomas Nelson titles may be purchased in bulk for educational, business, fundraising, or sales promotional use. For information, please email SpecialMarkets@ThomasNelson.com.

ISBN 978–1-4002–5013–4 (eBook)
ISBN 978–1-4002–5012–7 (HC))

All emphasis in Scripture quotations was added by the author.

This book is for informational purposes only and is not a substitute for professional advice, diagnosis, or treatment. It does not constitute or replace therapy, counseling, or mental health services. If you are experiencing mental health concerns, relationship challenges, or marital issues, please consult a licensed therapist, counselor, or qualified healthcare provider. Neither the author nor publisher are responsible for any outcomes resulting from the use of this material.

HarperCollins Publishers, Macken House, 39/40 Mayor Street Upper, Dublin 1, D01 C9W8, Ireland (https://www.harpercollins.com)

Library of Congress Cataloging-in-Publication Data

Names: TerKeurst, Lysa author | Muddamalle, Joel author | Cress, Jim author
Title: Surviving an unwanted divorce : a biblical, practical guide to letting go while holding yourself together / Lysa TerKeurst with Dr. Joel Muddamalle and Jim Cress.
Description: Nashville, Tennessee : Nelson Books, [2025] | Summary: "Lysa TerKeurst, Dr. Joel Muddamalle, and Licensed Professional Counselor Jim Cress, hosts of the Therapy & Theology podcast, help readers understand what the Bible says about how to survive the death of a marriage while pursuing wholeness and healing"-- Provided by publisher.
Identifiers: LCCN 2025025616 (print) | LCCN 2025025617 (ebook) | ISBN 9781400250127 hardcover | ISBN 9781400250134 ebook
Subjects: LCSH: Divorce--Biblical teaching | Divorce--Religious aspects--Christianity
Classification: LCC BS680.D62 T47 2025 (print) | LCC BS680.D62 (ebook) | DDC 248.8/46--dc23/eng/20250805
LC record available at https://lccn.loc.gov/2025025616
LC ebook record available at https://lccn.loc.gov/2025025617Printed in the United States of America

25 26 27 28 29 LBC 5 4 3 2 1

Contents

A Note from Lysa

When things were falling apart with my marriage, I felt like I had been in the equivalent of a serious head-on collision and desperately needed to go to an emergency room. The intensity of the pain and the severity of the trauma made it seem like I was emotionally bleeding out. After all, a part of me had just been severed . . . cut off . . . ripped apart. If my injuries had been physical, someone would have called 911 and the ambulance workers would have attempted to stabilize me and get me to the hospital. The ER trauma doctors would have known what to do to get my pain under control and take me into surgery to fix what had been severed. But there wasn't that level of care and help immediately available to me with the emotional trauma I was experiencing. No doctor could surgically fix my broken heart.

What would have helped me, in my pain and confusion, was a book like this. And, honestly, what has continued to help my healing post-divorce has been writing this very resource you now hold in your hands.

Please know from the start that I still wish there was no need for a book titled *Surviving an Unwanted Divorce*. The devastation of an unwanted divorce is horrific. So in no way, shape, or form do I ever want to glorify divorce or make it seem as if it's an easy solution to marriage difficulties. If you and your spouse are both willing to make the necessary changes with humble hearts and there is hope for you to get your marriage to a healthy place, please fight for that relationship.

But I know personally that sometimes that is just not possible. When the destruction and devastation have reached a point where you are now facing the death of your marriage, you need a resource like this. It's written not just from my personal experiences but also from the wisdom of trained professionals to help you navigate everything you are dealing with, both emotionally and spiritually.

While this book isn't an ultimate resource that will help you know what to do and what to say at every turn, my prayer is that this book will start to give you the emotional fortitude and biblical confidence to work through what you walk through along the way. Whether you're in the throes of a divorce, still processing things that happened years ago, or helping someone you love through a devastating season, this book is for you.

In full transparency, I feared writing a book like this would make it seem I am pro divorce. Please know, I am not that. I am pro healthy marriages and I am pro helping women who desperately need the support and information in this book. And, sister, if that is you, you are worth it.

Finally, I should also mention that certainly there are men on the receiving end of marriage devastation, too, and I hate that the Enemy is tearing families apart in every which way he can. I'll mostly be addressing other women throughout this book, because that is the experience I'm writing from. But I hope the principles help you, regardless of who you are.

I'm so grateful to be able to hand you this resource and tell you with full confidence that God loves you and you don't have to walk this road alone.

Introduction

Secrets Always Take a Toll on Their Keeper

Hello, my name is Lysa, and I have experienced a divorce. For a long while, I couldn't say those words. I couldn't wrap my brain around the word *divorce* being attached to my life. So my therapist, Jim, told me to say "the death of my marriage." That helped. But just changing the phraseology didn't change the intensity of my shock and pain.

I remember the night when I first knew the end was near. I was trying to process what had happened that day. I wasn't crying. And it felt weird that I wasn't slumped over and sobbing. I'm not sure if it was because I'd run out of tears. Or maybe holding back the tears gave me a sense of control to keep me from falling apart. Or maybe I wasn't crying because there was relief in finally knowing what was really true. But as quickly as I felt the relief of the truth, it was followed by a fear of finality.

Clarity didn't give me comfort. Clarity did, however, allow

me to see what I needed to see in order to know what I needed to do.

I was sitting on my bed, staring out the window. I couldn't take my eyes off the night sky. But I wasn't looking at the darkening scenery. I wasn't really looking outward at all. I was making my way through the internal realizations I'd resisted for so long. Instead of shoving them away, I let the thoughts of divorce stay with me. And I hated those thoughts. But staying in this marriage just wasn't an option any longer.

The dysfunctional dance had ramped back up. I knew the steps. I knew his promises were empty. I knew the vicious spins were starting again. I knew exactly where the choreography would take us. I knew nothing was going to magically make it all better this time. I knew the only way I could stay was if I was willing to pretend I didn't see what I saw. Pretend I didn't know what I now knew. And pretend that this level of ongoing heartbreak wasn't breaking me apart. But if I did that, his secrets would have to become my secrets. And I wasn't willing to do that.

Jim, my counselor, who had always been careful to let me come to my own conclusions, had taught me that we are as sick as our secrets. That statement got my attention! Before seeing Jim and another counselor I worked with, I thought I was being a good wife when I kept secret my suspicions and the later revelations of alarming things happening. Part of it was because, in the early stages of my marriage imploding, I didn't yet have solid proof of what I feared. But then, even when I made more and more discoveries, I still kept them secret from mostly everyone because I was riddled with fear, and I didn't know who I could trust to help me. I also knew the consequences of his choices wouldn't affect just him but our entire family. So, in my mind, I hadn't been keeping secrets; I had been trying to keep our world together and make hugely challenging choices in a situation I was ill-equipped to handle.

But holding all this inside me was making me sick, physically and emotionally. I didn't need to tell everyone, but I should have told some trusted people who could have helped me think through this more clearly. By trying to protect our marriage, I wound up not protecting myself. By not revealing the secrets, I was actually paying a very high cost.

There really are no free secrets.

They all have a cost, an impact, a toll that they take on their keeper.

By not saying anything, I was, in essence, preventing him from facing the consequences of his choices, which, looking back, I can see was not at all helpful. Yes, it temporarily protected me and our kids from what we would suffer if he was exposed. But we eventually paid an even greater cost because of how long that secrecy strung things out and how much worse it got in that time.

Sometimes stepping in and preventing natural consequences gets in the way of God using those consequences to bring about some sort of repentance.

Again, I'm not talking about telling everyone what's going on and inviting public opinion into your very private world. But telling the right people is crucial. If we think we're honoring our husbands by not doing this, we are, essentially, honoring what is dishonorable. So, when Jim told me that secrets can make people sick, I realized I had not been protecting our marriage. I had actually been preventing us both from getting the help we desperately needed.

But please understand, I get the fear of telling others. I get the fear of what it could unleash in your life. And I get the need to take the time to count the cost on both sides of this choice. Only you can make this decision. I just wish I would have told others sooner than I did. I think I prolonged my suffering and missed an earlier opportunity for me to hand him over to God and stop the madness of trying to change him myself.

Do you recognize yourself in my story? Have you caught yourself saying any of these things?

> "I just don't understand why he can't see what I see."
> "I can't wrap my brain around why he's doing this."
> "I would never do this to someone I loved."
> "How can he not know what breaking apart our family will do to our children?"

It's taken me a long time to come to grips with statements and questions like these. Of course you don't understand it. Because you don't think like he thinks. You aren't doing what he is doing. And you aren't blinded by the same behaviors he is engaging in.

Unhealthy choices will never make sense to a healthy person. And health has a very hard time bonding with unhealth. You can't make sense of things that make no sense. You can't make normal outcomes from dysfunctional ingredients. You can't bring into order someone who is constantly drawn to chaos. And you can't walk forward hand in hand with someone who is going in the opposite direction. At some point, the connection will slip, and though you're desperately grasping to hang on, their determination to pull away wins.

Unhealthy choices will never make sense to a healthy person.

When I finally did get my counselor Jim involved, he started to equip me with therapeutic insights to help me better understand what I was really dealing with. One day, he held up a glass with water in it and said, "Water seeks its own level." He put the glass on a table and pointed out how the water on the left side of the glass was even with the water on the right side of the glass. The only way to keep one side higher than the other was to tilt the glass. But that tilted glass would never be stable enough to stand without crashing over. In the same way, if one of the two people in a relationship is striving to make the relationship healthier but the other refuses, there is a high probability that the instability will lead to a crash.

It's a fool's game to drink the poison someone keeps giving you and hope that there are enough other good aspects in your relationship that you'll survive it.

By the time that night came, when I was staring out the window I understood this reality and had started to gain the emotional fortitude to take the hardest step of my life. Even though I knew this was the step I needed to take, I felt more alone than I'd ever felt. And all I wanted to do was to text my then-husband and ask him to come back home. For my entire adult life, he had been the one I wanted with me when I was processing something hard. He had been (as far as I knew) as invested in what affected me as I was. I always thought we would carry life's hardships *together*, figure it out *together*, and get through it *together*. So, of course, I wanted to text him.

But I'd been in this place before. Afraid. Lonely. Minimizing what kept happening. Missing him. Thinking things would surely be different this time. Giving in. Texting him. Getting a jolt of hope when he texted back all the words I'd hoped he would say. Believing the love bombing was true evidence of him changing. Taking him back. Enjoying a short season of reconciliation. Letting my guard down. Feeling a sense of safety and hope again.

Then the weird feeling that something was off again would start. The fears, the suspicions, the searching for evidence, being told I was crazy and wondering if I really was, in fact, crazy. Confrontation would lead to life turning upside down again, I would feel like I could barely function, and hopelessness would envelop me.

And here I was again.

Right back at another ground zero.

That's when the tears came. I put my phone in the drawer of my nightstand and rolled over in the darkness, where a fitful night of very little sleep awaited me. There would be a cost to finally saying *no more*. The fact that he could no longer be my person was one of the many costs I would have to pay for finally making the decision to leave. But the cost of continuing to stay was more than my body, mind, and heart could afford to keep paying. I wasn't giving up. I was finally accepting the reality that changing a marriage really isn't possible if one of the two people is unwilling or incapable of making the desperately needed changes. So I drew the finish line and stepped over into this terrifying unknown. I wrote this in my journal during that season:

> I have so much fear. I am heartbroken and devastated. I tried for years to prevent the reality I'm now living. I feel awful and lost and intensely alone. And it's even worse when I'm in a crowded room. That's actually the loneliest place for me, because I can hear the buzz of other people who like their lives and it's unsettling. I used to be one of them, who had a general sense of where my life was headed, but I was wrong. I used to love looking forward to the future. Now it just seems to be a dark blur of uncertainty. I want to move forward. But where do I go? Which direction is forward? What does

it even look like to be a Christian woman who is headed toward divorce?

Getting to the place where I finally was able to make the decision to divorce was a long process.

In 2016 I realized my then-husband was being unfaithful. In 2017 I announced we were divorcing. In 2018 we tried to reconcile, got a lot of counseling, and renewed our vows. In 2019 I started sensing things weren't right again. And it's been almost six years since I realized my marriage wasn't going to make it.

The process and time frames will look different for each person. Maybe you're still in the thick of heartbreaking discoveries or realizations that you are in a destructive marriage and aren't sure what to do. Or maybe you are in the very messy middle of a divorce. Or maybe you've made the brave decision to continue processing and healing from the fallout from your divorce years ago. Whatever your circumstances are, I'm so glad you're here. I know firsthand how long and painful the journey is. But I hope you will find a friend in me throughout the pages of this book, as you experience the healing and redemption you may have determined would never be possible for you.

I'm thankful to be in a different reality now. Because I'm in a different season, there's a part of me that just wants to move on and leave all this divorce stuff in my past. But almost every week I get another message about a woman's life being ripped apart by secrets she didn't know her husband was keeping. Or her husband's temper has reached a place where his verbal abuse or abuse of any kind is crushing her. Or his hidden spending habits on activities that aren't in keeping with their marriage vows have stolen her family's ability to pay the bills and he's refusing to stop the financial betrayal. Or there are things happening with him that she's afraid to tell anyone, because he's told her over and over that she didn't see what she saw or she didn't hear what she heard. His gaslighting has her starting to believe that she's the crazy one. Or she tried to confide in someone after he pinned her against a wall and broke his hand by punching a hole in the wall, but they made it seem like it was all her fault with statements like "Don't trigger him," "Don't instigate any hard conversations," "You should be having more sex with him," and "What could you do better so he will act better at home?"

Whatever the toxic dynamics are, we need to remember, like my friend Leslie Vernick taught me, there is a big difference between a difficult marriage and a destructive marriage. A difficult marriage is a good reason to go to counseling and marriage conferences to work on things together. A destructive marriage is a whole different beast.

This is a somber place to start a book. But if I'm not honest about where I was, your broken heart won't trust me enough to walk you on from here. More than teaching you anything right now, I want you to feel understood. That's why I'm so glad you're here. Rather than googling late at night trying to figure out what to do now, I hope you can find what you need in these pages. You are walking through a significant, life-altering tragedy. And I want you to know you're not alone.

I'm inviting two people along for this journey who helped me the most throughout my own path. My counselor, Jim Cress, who you'll be hearing from at the end of each chapter in the "Counselor's Corner," and a theologian friend, Dr. Joel Muddamalle, who you'll hear from throughout this book. If you've recently been hurt by a man in your life, I hope Joel's and Jim's biblical wisdom and tender voices of encouragement will be redeeming for you. I can't wait for you to learn from them!

Together, we want to take your hand and lead you to real wisdom, help you walk further in your healing journey, and equip you with solid biblical truth. Whether your story is very similar to mine or the reasons for your divorce are different, we want to enter the story of your healing. We want to help you find your way.

I want to make a few special notes so I make sure to include all who could benefit from this message. Certainly, like I said before, those of you in the messy middle of discovering infidelity and marriage implosion leading to divorce, this book is for you. But it's also for those of you whose spouse didn't cheat on you but instead broke your marriage vows in other destructive ways. We will get to this specifically in chapter 4, "Is the Only Valid Reason for Divorce Sexual Infidelity?" I pray that having Dr. Joel unpack the scriptures that have possibly confused you or left you feeling like leaving your emotionally destructive marriage wasn't biblically justified will ease the burden of shame you may be carrying.

This book is also for those of you whose divorce happened years ago and the intensity of the hurt isn't as all-consuming as it once was. The best way I can describe why this book will help you is to give you a mental picture one of my daughter's tutors once showed me. She held up a chart of all the building-block lessons a child has to master in order to be successful as they move through the higher grades. My daughter had missed some building-block basics, which was making moving forward challenging once she hit middle school. The tutor helped her go back to get a solid footing built in her educational pyramid. It took time to accomplish this, but once she did, her school experience improved immensely. I believe this book will be like that building-block exercise for you.

And, finally, this book is for the friend who wants to better understand how to help another friend facing a divorce. Read this book alongside her. Process it with her. And seek to understand what she's going through so you can support her. She doesn't need to face any of this alone, and you can be one of the most important people God uses in her life right now. You don't have to come up with all the wisdom. Just join her in reading this book so you can learn alongside her.

For whatever reason you're picking up this book, I'm so glad you're here. And while I can't promise you'll get the answers you want about what happened, I can help you find the answers you need to move on in healthier ways from here.

CHAPTER 1

A House Cut in Two

In the years before my marriage imploded, my friends and I (Lysa) were not talking about the things Jim, Joel, and I now address on our podcast, *Therapy & Theology*. We didn't have the language for what we were experiencing then. We didn't know how to talk about the vast array of personality disorders that can severely complicate typical marital issues. We didn't know how to recognize the dysfunctional patterns of addictions, gaslighting, and emotional abuse, or how much the body is affected by emotional trauma.

But let's be honest. Very few of us were going to counseling then.

At the time, I was in the throes of raising five kids and was unaware of some very concerning patterns in my marriage. I had gotten used to the dysfunction I was living in. So, as a good Christian girl, I lived by the mantra that as long as I loved my husband, respected him, and was determined to encourage him rather than confront him, I was doing what I could to keep my marriage on track. And I also kept thinking that the stress of raising kids would lessen as they got older and things would adjust in good ways.

Loving, respecting, and encouraging are all good, biblical actions to take toward another person. But other things were happening, too, and we really could have used someone trained to help us. Not to mention the fact that I was contributing to our issues by playing the role of a codependent enabler.

Don't miss that. I was contributing to the dysfunction.

But, again, I didn't know that. What I did know was that I kept getting this sinking feeling that something was off. There were things that just didn't make sense.

Once, in the middle of the night, I woke up from a dead sleep with a compelling sense I needed to walk to the kitchen right at that very minute. My then-husband was in the kitchen and got startled when he realized I was standing in the doorway looking at him. He quickly shoved a device into the pocket of the shorts he was wearing. I asked him what it was, and, without missing a beat, he told me it was a remote control. I knew that wasn't the truth, so I asked to see it. He refused, and an argument ensued that left me feeling like the crazy one once again. I remember going back to bed feeling like I was living in the middle of a bad dream. My head was spinning, and my heart was racing so fast that I barely slept that night.

Why didn't I call someone that next day? Why didn't I sound the alarm with a trusted friend and ask for help? Why didn't I reach out to a counselor or our pastor or one of his friends who could help me get to the bottom of this?

I don't know.

I guess a part of me was afraid that if I was wrong, I would be giving him a story to use against me to prove that he was, in fact, living with a crazy woman. The very thought of investigating my husband felt incredibly dishonoring, wrong, and scary. Plus, if he discovered that I was investigating, it would probably cause extreme turmoil in our marriage. And if my suspicions were incorrect, it could make me look like a jealous fool instead of a wife who just wanted the truth. Another part of me feared people wouldn't believe me because he was such a well-respected person at that time. But the biggest factor of all was that I didn't want what I suspected to be true, because then I would have to face realities that absolutely terrified me.

If I believed it was a remote control, that night was just an incident when I got confused and he got frustrated.

If I believed it was a phone I hadn't seen him using before, that night was going to flip our family's world upside down and prove some of my greatest fears were coming true.

So I kept quiet.

Throughout that year, I did look for that "remote control," but I never found it. And all the many times we went on date nights, did family devotions together, went on fun vacations, had meaningful conversations while walking hand in hand, and snuggled up to watch the news at night and catch up on how our days had been gave me enough of a sense of normalcy that I started feeling terribly guilty for my suspicions.

Round and round I went that year, feeling like the problem was me, until I felt like the problem was him, until I felt like the problem was me again, until I felt like the problem was what I sometimes feared it might be.

I remember someone telling me once that the devil always overplays his hand. In other words, sin may stay hidden for a while, but it will eventually be exposed. Now, I realize some people never get the proof of exactly what their husband did.

But please remember something Jim taught me: "Where there is smoke there is fire." Maybe you won't get the full picture of what he did, but give it some time and he will eventually expose his character. Sometimes that takes a really long time. For me, it took a year from that night in the kitchen.

That next year, the weekend of our daughter's wedding, I finally found the device, and it was, in fact, a burner phone my then-husband was using to stay in contact with his affair partner. I confronted him, and he finally acknowledged there was someone else. I'll spare you the details of everything else he said, the justifications and downplaying and gaslighting. But, suffice it to say, despite all my keeping quiet and trying very hard to maintain the peace in our relationship, some of my worst fears were realized.

Maybe you have had a similar experience of feeling like you were crazy until you realized it was all part of a cover-up. I'm not sure how your story played out. Whether there was an affair or there were other destructive realities in your marriage, I want you to have this moment where I clearly and definitively assure you that I believe you. I believe how hard you tried. I believe you did what you could and probably a whole lot more to save your marriage. I believe this isn't what you wanted.

There are too many of us who love Jesus, who were desperate to keep our families together, who couldn't stop the confusing things that were happening behind closed doors with our spouse, who endured things we should never have experienced, who begged God to make things different but, in the end, found ourselves staring at divorce papers anyway.

Are there things you and I need to own? Mistakes we made? Things we said out of anger and frustration? Demonstrations of codependency? Was there enabling? For me, yes—absolutely yes.

And those would have been great reasons for us to go get counseling to address what we were both contributing. But was I a faithful wife who wanted to do anything I possibly could to have a good marriage? Yes.

And I suspect you were too.

Imperfect? Yes. Deserving of what happened? No.

In North Carolina, the state where we lived, you have to wait a year and a day from the time you separate until you can file for divorce. So I decided to use that year to see what would happen if I completely removed myself from the equation of my husband's decision-making. I stopped warning him about what could happen to our family. I stopped preventing the consequences of his choices. I stopped trying to fix what was beyond my ability to fix. And, instead, I used that year to work on my own healing.

Removing my influence from his life gave me an opportunity to be an observer rather than a savior. In the end, I got the clarity I needed. It wasn't the clarity I wanted, but it did inform the decisions I then knew I needed to make. When I called my attorney to let her know it was time to file, I felt like I was having an out-of-body experience. My physical self was saying words my emotional self still couldn't fully process. I had worked so long to keep things together, and now I would be signing on to the severing required to live a life separate from him.

I had begged God to open his eyes and make him want our family. To make him see all he was giving up.

Why couldn't he feel the angst of all the treasured traditions we'd no longer enjoy together?

Why couldn't he foresee all the major life events our kids and grandkids would now have to navigate between two separate parents, two separate homes, two separate lives?

Why couldn't he play out the future consequences that would

continue to cause challenges and heartbreak and rippling emotional effects for all of us for years to come?

The picture that kept coming to my mind was a man and a woman standing in front of the house they once shared as it was cut in half. He wanted the left side. She would get the right side. So a massive chainsaw split it right down the middle and pulled it apart. The man who wanted his half got that. But he hadn't factored in all the internal connections being severed that caused so many other things to malfunction. Split pipes causing water to spill out everywhere. The gas lines becoming dangerously exposed. The house being open to the elements and the foundation no longer being solid.

Of course, over time, and maybe with the right help from people who know how to fix each broken thing, repairs could be made. But that home would never be the same. Chances are, it would all have to be torn down, and the loss would be massive.

The loss. The massive loss. Why hadn't he factored that in? Or, worse, if he did factor it in, how in the world was anything worth this price?

Those maddening questions with no answers ushered in many sleepless nights and a sense of dread for each new day. But, deep in my heart, one of the most haunting questions of all was *Why was I not enough for him?* Please don't read that as a pitiful pleading. It wasn't that. It was more of a deep wrestling within me. I kept drawing a straight line from his rejection to my insecurities.

Each of us has things about us we wish were different. I'm not going to dignify those nagging negative statements we make about ourselves by listing them here. I know what mine are. And you know yours. It can seem so logical to think that if those things about us were different, our marriages would have turned out differently. And, while I'm all about working to become the healthiest version of ourselves, it's not helpful to mentally beat ourselves up and reduce our worth down to the sum total of our flaws.

But sometimes it's not just the insecurities we feel; it's all the negativity spoken over us that feels like confirmation of our worst thoughts about ourselves. Our own insecurities trickle in and out of our thought life. But then someone whose opinion really matters to us voices that same negativity over us, and suddenly it becomes cemented into a belief we have about ourselves. Then, when other hard situations occur, we circle back to this faulty belief about ourselves and see this as further proof that we are, indeed, not enough. Or, even worse, that we really are the crazy, broken wife not worth staying with and fighting for.

You know what's really sad, looking back? I was allowing this man, who had lied to me over and over, to be a voice of truth in my life about my worth. Please read that sentence again: *I was allowing this man, who had lied to me over and over, to be a voice of truth in my life about my worth.* If he couldn't tell the truth about where he was going, who he was seeing, what he was doing, and why he was being distant and cold, why on earth did I think he would be a good candidate for telling me the truth about me? And if his best thinking got him into this place where he could justify leaving our family, then his best thinking about me should not be factored into a true assessment of my worth and mental health.

Even if you are not struggling with your worth right now, you will probably encounter statements spoken to you and about you during this season that can make you question things about yourself. I had to spend a lot of time in counseling, untangling what was true and not true about me. It was crucial not just so I could heal from the past but so I could move forward into my future. Many of those therapeutic practices we'll get into later in this book, but here's the deal: We have to consider the source each time someone speaks something over us as an assessment of who we are or the decisions we've made.

I feel so stinking protective over what you allow to be spoken over you right now, when your feelings are tender and your heart is broken. Here's a good rule of thumb: If it's coming from a trusted person, whose pure desire is to seek your highest good, and they come to you in humility and grace, by all means, consider what they are saying. But if it's spoken over you by someone with an ulterior motive, be very cautious about taking that into your head and heart.

A line spoken over us can easily become a lie we believe, which can turn into a label we put on ourselves. Those labels we put on ourselves can then turn into liabilities in all of our future relationships.

> A line spoken over us can easily become a lie we believe, which can turn into a label we put on ourselves.

This is important to recognize and to untangle.

You don't have to put pressure on yourself to untangle every lie and get to the root of every issue, though I hope our journey together through these pages will help untangle a few. But whatever the circumstances are with your heartbreak, can you agree with me on a few things?

- When you're walking toward an unwanted divorce, your husband was obviously no longer seeking your highest good.
- Some of the words he spoke to you might have been motivated by a negative narrative he wrote about you in his

mind. This negative narrative may not be true, but it's what he has to say in order to justify what he is doing.

- Sometimes people living in sin change their definition of truth to whatever protects their bad behavior and not what is in keeping with the facts.
- Sometimes you will get blamed for choices your ex made that have nothing to do with you at all. That responsibility is not yours to carry. Brokenness in them is not always evidence of brokenness in you.
- There is a spiritual battle here. Never forget God has a plan, but the Enemy has a plan too. The Enemy wants to steal, kill, and destroy (John 10:10), and one of his most effective tactics is destroying families.

Make no mistake: Divorce and what leads to divorce are personal. But we should not personalize every aspect of what's happening, because there are other things going on. Some we're aware of and some we're not. Maybe some parts have to do with you, but not all parts have to do with you. And it's easy to forget that.

When we remember these things, we can start seeing our circumstances more clearly and recognizing the difference between a truth and a lie more readily and stop personalizing so much of what happened.

You are worth so much more than a house cut in two.

You are worth so much more than a man who tried to break you because he himself was so very broken.

You are worth laying down the defeating statement of "I am not enough" and replacing it with "I became more than he deserved."

COUNSELOR'S CORNER WITH JIM

I have seen so much confusion around the word *codependency*. I find that people seem to either overuse the word or underuse it. I would define *codependency* as "compassion taken too far." Compassion is good until it turns into trying to fix someone else.

So if codependency is taking compassion too far, let's break down the word *compassion*. *Com* is a prefix that carries the meaning of being "with." *Passion* can be defined in one aspect as "to suffer" (think of the Passion of Christ). So *compassion* literally means "to suffer with."[1] The preposition *with* is very important here. We can sit *with* a loved one who is suffering, but our responsibility is not to suffer *for* someone else.

In Galatians 6:2, the apostle Paul instructs us to "bear one another's burdens." Then, in verse 5, Paul reminds us, "For each will have to bear his own load" (ESV). This can be confusing, because it can seem conflicting. The word pictures here in Koine Greek help clear things up. The word for "burdens" in Galatians 6:2 is *barei*. This refers to a person who is overloaded with a weight too heavy to carry by oneself.[2] So when Paul calls us to bear one another's burdens, he's calling us to help when the other person is overloaded and shouldn't be carrying that much weight. In Galatians 6:5, however, the Greek word for "load" is *phortion*. This is a different term that carries the meaning of a ship's regular, normal cargo load, or a soldier's knapsack.[3] So we are called to bear our own loads when they're regular burdens that we are meant to carry ourselves.

Often in codependency, especially in close relationships, one person is working hard to help carry the regular burden that belongs solely to another person. *Maybe if I try harder, my spouse will change. Maybe if I do ______, my spouse will stop drinking, quit looking at pornography, or stop verbally and emotionally abusing me.* Always remember, you cannot be the external solution to someone else's internal problem.

Here's one way codependency plays out: "I need you to be okay, so I can be okay. So, how can I help you be okay, so I can feel okay, because I want to feel okay, okay?" Do you see this pattern of the codependent person trying to self-regulate by attempting to regulate another person?

I have found that many Christian women find themselves in this codependent cycle without even realizing it. Many of my clients who are well meaning and who so desire to have a godly marriage will inadvertently become codependent when they subscribe to the kind of mindset that says, "If you want to make sure to keep your marriage a priority, his needs have to take priority over your needs." Or, in more severe cases, they take the word *submit* in the Bible to mean they can have no needs at all. They interpret the call for wives to submit in Ephesians 5:22 to mean there are no biblical grounds for them to draw boundaries with a husband who is hurting them.

The other message Christian women sometimes hear on repeat inside their minds is "You are biblically required to respect him no matter what. And if you want love, you first must give him respect." But nowhere in Scripture does God call us to honor what is dishonorable to Him. Respecting your husband can be a good thing until that word gets twisted into meaning you have to do the dysfunctional dance of codependent enabling. Respecting him should not mean that you cover things up for him so he appears more respectable to others than he really is.

The goal of addressing codependency is not to be cured of it but to have more and more self-awareness to know when you're close to the line of taking things like compassion, respect, and submission too far.

If all this sounds familiar, let me just say, with all tenderness, that it is so natural and understandable that you were trying to do this from a heart of care. Your motive was good in trying to protect your family. And you were trying to honor and respect your husband ultimately so you could be a really good wife. Instead of mentally beating yourself up, let's use this information to be more self-aware now. Remember, self-awareness often leads to self-compassion.

If you've been codependent in the past, confess it to God and forgive yourself. Remind yourself: If you were faithful in your marriage, you honored your part of the marital contract and covenant. Surrender your spouse or ex-spouse to God. And then take a step to actively lay down that codependency. Here's a good script to say to yourself in an act of laying it down and regaining your ability to focus on working on yourself instead of other people: "I didn't cause it. I can't control it. I can't cure it."[4]

CHAPTER 2

What About My Covenant with God?

I (Joel) have never experienced the death of my marriage, but I've had a front-row seat to the extreme complexities and hardships in my own parents' marriage and also the tragedy of divorce in my extended family. Even more heartbreaking for me and my wife, we have friends who got married around the same time as we did, and the vast majority are no longer together.

As I look at the why behind all this tragedy, I see a common thread running through these stories: the presence of sin that often expresses itself through addictions, selfish actions, and, ultimately, a disregard for the image of God that we represent. We'll get into more about this in just a moment.

But first, yes, I am the theologian who will bring biblical perspectives and insights to this journey. But more importantly, I need to let you know that my heart is very sensitive to the realities you are facing. When you are in a tender place, you need to hear from a tender voice, and my commitment to you is to be just that.

Though this is a book about the death of a marriage, we need to start by understanding that a marriage is made up of two individual people. Two individual image bearers of God. That is the biblical foundation we need to hold on to as we continue through these pages. What does it mean to be an image bearer? To answer that question, we need to understand an important theological principle called the *imago Dei*. That's a fancy Latin phrase simply translated as "the image of God."

I would personally define the image of God as an irrevocable status given to humanity as a gift that marks us and separates us from other created things as royal children of the King. In other words, only humankind gets the gift of being made in the image of God. And no other creature or creation is given this gift. Theologian Herman Bavinck said it this way: "Nothing in a human being is excluded from the image of God. While all creatures display vestiges of God, only a human being is the image of God."[1] In other words, all of creation in some way points to the beauty of God, but only humankind puts on display the full brilliance of God's image.

The key Scripture reference for this is Genesis 1:26–28:

> God said, "Let us make man in our *image*, according to our *likeness*. They will rule the fish of the sea, the birds of the sky, the livestock, the whole earth, and the creatures that crawl on the earth." *So God created man in his own image; he created him in the image of God; he created them male and female.* God

blessed them, and God said to them, "Be fruitful, multiply, fill the earth, and subdue it. Rule the fish of the sea, the birds of the sky, and every creature that crawls on the earth." (CSB)

Hang with me here. I promise I'm not going to go too academic on you, but we need to explore some of these foundational biblical contexts so you have the full understanding of what God wants you to know. Having this understanding will be a great comfort to your soul. And it can also be a source of reassuring truth for others who are forced to walk a path toward an unwanted divorce.

I'd love to draw our attention to two Hebrew words in the passage above, *tselem* and *demuth*, translated into English as "image" (*tselem*) and "likeness" (*demuth*). These words held rich meaning in the Ancient Near Eastern world (the social, historical, and cultural context of the Old Testament). They were used to describe human royalty and their relationship to the divine.[2]

Let's slow down and read what the text actually says. Who was made in the image of God? Just Adam? No. Just Eve? No. They were both, male and female, made in the image of God. This means that these two individuals, who would eventually come into a covenant marriage, were first image bearers of God and therefore the royal children of the King of heaven and earth. We could say it this way: In the chronology of events, Adam and Eve were first created as image bearers. Then, they came together as God established the institution of marriage. And this order matters.

Keeping this in mind, if a divorce is the death of a marriage, let's dive into the birth of a marriage. What was God's design and intent for this sacred relationship?

The English word *marriage* is rooted in the Hebrew word

berith, which is also translated as a "covenant." Marriage is the union of one man and one woman in a covenant commitment to each other (Proverbs 2:17; Jeremiah 31:32; Ezekiel 16:8, 59, 60; Malachi 2:14). Part of being in a covenant relationship includes covenant requirements for both parties. We could think of this in terms of a contract between two individuals. This is how the ancient Israelites understood it and how the rabbis taught and interpreted the law in regard to it. Contracts require payments, stipulations, and penalties for stipulations that are broken. Let's break down what these looked like in the Jewish understanding of the Old Testament.

- **PAYMENT.** In order for a marriage to take place, the husband had to bring a dowry. This was a payment he brought to give to the woman! In other words, even after they got married, the dowry belonged to the woman. But the control of the finances from a practical level would still be under the husband's stewardship. That's why the certificate of divorce was so important.
- **STIPULATION.** Every contract has terms for what each person fulfills and benefits from. In the context of marriage, the husband brought safety and security through financial, spiritual, and emotional support. And the wife was to bring safety and security through how she managed the house and cared for the needs of everyone within the family. The bottom line was that both parties had something to bring to the marriage. If one didn't bring those things, that broke the contract. All broken contracts have consequences.
- **PENALTIES.** The consequences for broken contracts varied. Divorce was not intended to be the first recourse. It was not the only option. The rabbis had a process in place to

> try to help the people in the marriage reconcile. This meant both parties, in humility, had to do their part. But if the husband was stubborn, unwilling to change, and left the marriage in a state of utter destruction, there was protection built in for the woman, in getting a certificate of divorce (Deuteronomy 24:1–4, Matthew 5:31, Matthew 19:7 and Mark 10:4).[3]

The certificate of divorce was a public declaration that the woman was not the one in the wrong, so she could be welcomed back into the community with dignity and honor.[4] Another reason the certificate of divorce helped the woman was that it allowed her to reclaim her dowry, to take personal possession of it, so she wouldn't become financially destitute after her husband left her.

If a woman didn't have the certificate of divorce, not only did she risk public shunning, but it put her family at risk for public shame as well. In some cases like this, the family would turn their back on the woman so they could stay in good standing with the community. This was incredibly tragic, because without their support and having no other financial means, she would potentially have to turn to something like prostitution for survival.[5] So you can see how crucial it was for the woman to get a certificate of divorce.[6]

You may be wondering why we are spending time talking about all this. It's because we want to highlight how seriously God views marriage. The concept of marriage was instituted by God and was first seen with Adam and Eve (Genesis 2:18–25). Later, in Matthew 19:6, we find that this union is framed within the context of covenant, and God's desire is for that covenant to be upheld and honored. What was His original plan for how this covenant should play out?

Marriage is to involve self-sacrifice through mutual submission. Paul unpacked this in Ephesians 5:20–21, stating, "Giving thanks always for everything to God the Father in the name of our Lord Jesus Christ, *submitting to one another in the fear of Christ*" (CSB). The idea here is that, when both individuals are living in holy reverence in light of Christ, they will come into unity as they are being led by Jesus. In other words, if a married couple finds themselves both submitting to Christ, they will find that there is also a natural impulse toward mutual submission to each other. One way this mutual submission might flourish is when both participants cultivate the fruit of the Spirit in their lives (Galatians 5:22–26). While the fruit of the Spirit is for all believers to exercise, there is something even more important about exercising the fruit of the Spirit in humility and love for each other in a marriage. This keeps each other's hearts soft and willing to sacrifice out of that love, which makes forgiveness so much easier.

As you can see, God has an ideal for marriage. And He wants us to uphold that ideal without putting another image bearer's safety, security, and well-being at risk. A great caution comes when the institution of marriage is placed above the safety, security, and well-being of the two image bearers who come together to form that marriage covenant. In the same way Jesus said that "the Sabbath was made for man and not man for the Sabbath" (Mark 2:27 CSB), God didn't create humanity for marriage, but rather marriage is a God-ordained institution that should always honor the image bearers within that marriage.

Marriage was created for humanity to point to the brilliant faithfulness of Christ and His love for His bride, the church. So when we elevate marriage itself above the dignity and safety of the image bearers in a marriage, we actually dishonor the picture of marriage that Christ puts on display with His love for

His bride. And this ultimately is what compels us to deal with the dysfunctions within a marriage, as our aim is to first and foremost bring honor to the Lord.

> Marriage is a God-ordained institution that should always honor the image bearers within that marriage.

For example, when well-meaning Christians encourage a woman caught in a marriage with destructive patterns to stay married at all costs, this is evidence that we've elevated the institution of marriage over the individual image bearer she is. What should happen is accountability for the individual acting in destructive ways, with the aim of restoring the ideal of God's intent for marriage. In so doing, there is correction for the one who is sinning and not shame for the one who needs to be rescued.

If all this is true, how do things get so out of whack sometimes?

There are certain things all Christians have a basic understanding of. For instance, the faithful covenant love of God toward His people. This is referred to as a *unilateral covenant*. The direction goes from God to us. God is the one who establishes and maintains that covenant. It is not because of or contingent on anything we do.[7] Things go sideways when we try to take what is true only of God's relationship with us and make that true of our human-to-human relationships. A covenant made between humans is different from the covenant between God and His people. A covenant between humans is called a *bilateral covenant*. This means both people have equal responsibility to uphold the stipulations in the covenant.

I've often heard people say, "But wait, marriage is a covenant between us and God." I've even heard women say, "Even if my husband broke the vows, I can't break my covenant with

God." I understand where these statements come from. As your theologian friend, maybe I can provide some clarity around this confusion.

Precision matters in our words. When you make your covenant promise with your spouse in marriage (bilateral), you do not make that covenant with God. In fact, it is something much more significant. You make that covenant in the presence of God as judge. What does this mean? It means that if one person breaks the covenant, there is more at risk because they made that promise acknowledging God as judge. This means they ultimately have to answer to God, who is the judge and witness of that covenant promise. Guess what? That judge is also the upholder of the innocent and the rescuer of the victim who was left holding the weight of something they were never intended to bear alone.

If you're feeling like you are that person, the one holding the full weight of your heartbreak, along with all the pressure to maintain normalcy for your kids, I want to share with you a few of my favorite New Testament verses, Matthew 11:28–29: "Come to me, all of you who are weary and burdened, and I will give you rest. Take my yoke upon you and learn from me, because I am lowly and humble in heart, and you will find rest for your souls" (CSB). This is so encouraging for me because it's a reminder that Jesus is right next to us. He is walking with us. And He won't abandon us on the way. There is rest for our souls.

One thing that may make you doubt this, though, is your worry about being a displeasure and disappointment to the Lord. This can happen when you've held some beliefs or have been told as gospel truth things that aren't actually in keeping with the full context of what God teaches. And that kind of biblical misinformation can breed shame inside you.

It's going to be much harder to take steps forward in healing if shame doesn't get untangled first. I have heard from way too many good Christian women who have been told either directly or passively that keeping their marriage together matters more than they do. It can be inappropriately celebrated that a woman stayed in a destructive marriage because people think God wants that more than her safety and security. It breaks my heart, and I believe God's heart, too, when other Christians shame a woman who has to accept the harsh reality of a divorce she did not want. You are not another statistic of a failed marriage. You are a woman who desperately wanted to please God, who finally realized she couldn't save her marriage all by herself.

Whether you are currently in the throes of an impending divorce or still walking the road of recovery post-divorce, my prayer for you right now is that you're able to finally exhale, knowing a failed marriage doesn't make you a failure in God's eyes.

Sister, I hope you now know how much God loves you. And making decisions to protect your dignity, safety, and security is the sign not of a weak-willed woman but of a woman of great courage and strength, who has finally said enough is enough.

I (Lysa) think now would be a good time for us both to do an exercise. Let's make some declarations out loud:

> I am not what I've done or what's been done to me.
> I am not the worst of what others have said about me.
> I am not just a woman who's experienced the death of her marriage.

I am a woman who loves God, and God loves me.
I am made in His image.
I am committed to the truth, and I will not engage with lies that try to come at me.
I am a reflection of the glory and goodness of God.
I am loved from the depth of God's unfathomable Father's heart.
I am treasured beyond imagination.

COUNSELOR'S CORNER WITH JIM

We all have life stories that affect how we see ourselves, our life circumstances, and what we can do about them. But more often than not, we don't take the time to unpack those stories with a trained counselor to gain a broader, clearer perspective on how we come to our various feelings and viewpoints. We need to tend well what we've been through in our lives, but we also need to bring to the surface conclusions we make and what we now tell ourselves because of what we've been through in the past. That's why I tell everyone I work with that we need to collect the dots, then connect the dots and correct the dots. We all have lived our lives in specific details, but we treat our life stories with vagueness. A powerful saying I borrow from my friend Nate Larkin is "What happens in vagueness, stays in vagueness." That's why I want to invite you to do a life-story exercise called "the Trauma Egg."[8]

The Trauma Egg is a powerful, practical tool I use in all my counseling intensives that addresses emotional trauma, as well as the impact of abuse, abandonment, and any unprocessed pain from the past. If you haven't done this exercise before, make sure to do it in a quiet, secluded, safe place. It should take three or more hours to thoroughly complete this life-story project.

This is how you can set up your Trauma Egg. First, get a poster board and several colored markers. Draw a giant egg shape on the board, leaving each of the four corners of the board empty. Next, in the top left corner of the poster board, write out some of the rules of the family you grew up in. You can list both spoken rules and unspoken rules. Remember, with kids, more is caught than taught. Here are some examples:

Don't make Mom or Dad mad.

Don't talk about family business outside of the home.

You're only successful if you make good grades.

Next, in the upper right corner of the poster board, list the different roles you played in your family of origin. These classic roles may include the mascot or entertainer, the hero, the rebel, the good boy or good girl, the scapegoat, the lost child, the peacekeeper or rescuer, the surrogate spouse to Mom or Dad, the responsible one, the honor-roll student, the athlete, and so forth.

Next, on the bottom left corner of your poster board, write out some of the adjectives that describe your father. These descriptive qualities can be from your childhood to your age today. Then use the bottom right corner of your poster board to list some of the adjectives describing your mother. I often find that those I counsel struggle with listing out these parental attributes. I tell them this part of the exercise is what I call "Naming, Not Blaming."

The four corners reveal the "setting" the Trauma Egg is in. Although our Trauma Eggs are not static and are ongoing, it's important to have the context of our family of origin as we process our own personal life experiences. I often say that if it's hysterical, it's historical.

Next, divide the inside of your Trauma Egg into equally sized small sections. Try to mark off twenty or more of these small sections. Then, starting at the first section, located at the bottom of the egg, draw a simple stick figure or symbol representing anything from your past that was painful, traumatic, abusive, negatively significant, sexual in any way, shaming, or sad. Then continue until you fill all the small sections. One tip is to make a cheat sheet on paper as you go, corresponding to the pictures and symbols in each square, so you don't forget what the symbols represent.

As you work on this, I invite you to utilize my FIT Principle to help you start making connections between the things you've added to your Trauma Egg. F stands for "facts": This is what happened to you. The I stands for "impact": This is how the specific facts impacted you. The T stands for

TRAUMA EGG EXAMPLE

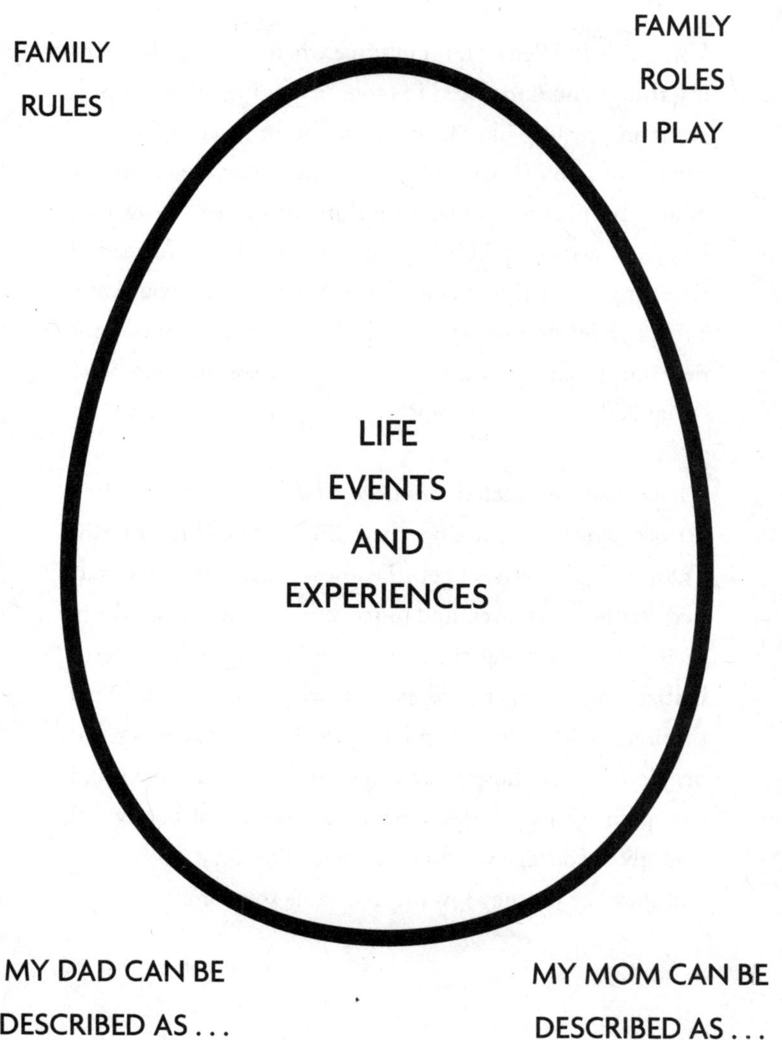

"track": This is a shame script or faulty belief that, through the Trauma Egg exercise, you might now see running throughout your life story.

Using this FIT lens, you might see where you may be owning things you don't need to own, managing other people's emotions, feeling like the constant victim, feeling like you can't count on other people, or thinking you aren't worthy of love and will never make anything of yourself. Now that you've identified and become more aware of this, instead of repeating this script over and over again, taking you down a track of defeat, say to yourself, "This is an opportunity for new life. What do I want to do to move forward from here? What is the next right step?"

I have had the sacred privilege of spending hours with people, slowly unpacking their life stories through this Trauma Egg exercise. I get to witness individuals and married couples discover and uncover unhealed wounds in their lives and bring them into the healing light of Jesus Christ and another safe person who walks with them through their stories. I regularly get to see these courageous people connect those sacred dots and find freedom from past pain, abuse, abandonment, rejection, and betrayal. I lovingly encourage you to go do your life story work today and start the journey toward that same freedom.

CHAPTER 3

But Doesn't God Hate Divorce?

I (Lysa) distinctly remember the first time I had to check the box that said "divorced" on a medical form asking for my marital status.

This moment isn't a fuzzy, faded memory. No, it is one of those memories that takes up residence and plays on repeat whenever something reminds me of that day. I would imagine no one else at the doctor's office has since given that day a second thought. But to me it was a marked moment. I see the gray-blue chairs with brown wooden arms in the waiting area. HGTV was playing on the television overhead with the volume turned all the way down. The gal behind the pull-back glass had black curly hair and was wearing blue scrubs and had a blue face mask on.

I stared down at the form. And though no one else was speaking, I could hear voices inside my mind that were laced with judgment. As I put the pen to the paper, everything in me wanted to write an explanation off to the side of this page: *"This was the most heart-wrenching experience of my life. I fought hard—really hard—to save my almost thirty-year marriage. I didn't rush this decision. It took me years. Years when our kids and I endured a lot. Things we shouldn't have seen, heard, and discovered. Things that weren't stopping. So I experienced one of the most painful losses I've ever known . . . the death of my marriage."*

But there wasn't space in that tiny box to put all that. So I just scratched the tip of the pen onto the paper in the shape of a checkmark beside the word *divorced*. And then I started to cry when one of the next lines asked me for my emergency contact.

This isn't true for everyone, but because I had it ingrained in my head that divorce should never be an option for a Christian couple, my new relationship status felt like a declaration that I was now less of a person, less of a Christ follower, less in my morality, less in my wisdom, and less trustworthy. It was like my ex-husband's choices had detonated, and the shrapnel had then marred *me* in every way.

I also felt that because infidelity and other secrets were attached to our marriage, they were now attached to me. I remember being in the shower and feeling desperate to scrub it all off. It was like I had wounds all over that were getting infected more and more by the minute. I needed to scrub them clean. I needed antiseptic ointment. I needed bandages. I needed a tourniquet. Something to stop me from bleeding out. But no matter how much I tried to clean my skin, no soap could reach what felt so gross.

Even more, nothing rubbed salt into the raw and tender places of my heart like the commentary people shared about my divorce. Some people were well meaning and genuinely concerned. Others had an air of superiority about them, as if my unwanted divorce somehow reduced me to someone to pity. Rather than simply offer compassion and help, some contributed to the pain by airing their opinions, accusations, and judgments. One ministry leader even warned people to stay away from me, as if my divorce was some kind of leprosy. My divorce opened the door for people to question things about me and to make assumptions that weren't true. Jim had warned me that people are usually down on what they aren't up on. Boy, was that true with some people.

I would think to myself, *If only they knew the whole story. They wouldn't say what they're saying. They wouldn't think what they are thinking. They wouldn't have sent the harsh DMs on social media. They wouldn't say such cruel things behind my back. They wouldn't say statements straight to my face, like "Well, you know there are two sides to every story" or "I would never give up on marriage. I don't believe in divorce."*

All this left me wondering, *Should I explain some of the harsh realities and reveal more of the story?*

But, then again, why would I entrust more details to people who were already proving they couldn't understand? They hadn't walked the dark paths I'd walked. They hadn't been close enough to me to see the whites of my eyes turn a blistering red and become swollen with agony over and over and over.

They didn't know.

They didn't feel what I was now feeling.

It hadn't hit them like it all hit me.

But the shock of what they were finding out definitely brought about lots of commentary. Even some close friends couldn't reconcile what they thought to be true about my then-husband and what was now coming to light. They had so many questions.

I get it. Because when I found out my ex-husband was living a double life, I couldn't process it either. Nothing made sense. Some things had seemed off at times, and his attitude wasn't as warm toward me in times of stress, but we were in a major season of transitioning our kids to college, with some of them even getting engaged. It was easy to attribute what didn't quite add up to those things. I'm just saying, most people looked at him and thought he was solid, including the counselor we were seeing at the time. So I did too.

But I was wrong.

I hadn't factored in the possibility that he might be building a facade of integrity. And that behind the scenes there was a whole secret world he was living in that I knew nothing about. And when I found out, I felt paralyzed because I thought, *People aren't going to believe me if I try to tell them what's going on.* And right behind that thought was, *They will wonder how I could have not known.* Shame became a powerful entanglement wrapped around every thought I had. *How could I have been so naive, so blind, so unaware?* I felt stupid. I felt ill-equipped to handle this. I felt so much shame that I didn't really know this man who I thought I knew better than anyone. I thought I was living a beautifully authentic life. And yet the more I pulled back the curtain, the more I discovered and the more I was stunned.

No one but me will ever know all that I felt, experienced, and was crushed by. And no one but you will ever know all of those realities for you either. It's so deeply complex and confusing, mind bending and heart wrenching. I'm not trying to be dramatic. I just want it clearly stated that divorce isn't just a decision a person makes one day. It's a vortex of indescribable pain, shame, confusion, and devastation wrapped in a tangle of questions that will never be answered and a heap of judgment from those who truly don't understand.

Maybe some people get divorced for much simpler reasons. But for most of the people I've talked to who have walked this road, there's nothing simple about it. And it is something we desperately don't want. For me, after many attempts at reconciliation and a vow renewal where I really thought things had finally turned around for good, the roller-coaster ride of all these ups and downs left me in a place where my brain just couldn't process all that God had allowed. And then, as divorce became more and more likely, the haunting words "God hates divorce" seemed like a dagger to my already fragile and disoriented heart.

If it was time to get off the roller-coaster ride and accept the reality that our marriage was over, what did that mean for me? What did that mean for me as a Christian woman? I had already faced the rejection of my then-husband. I had already faced the rejection of people who sided with him. Was I now going to also have to face the rejection of God? I had believed with all my heart that God would never leave me or forsake me. But was divorce the one thing that might cause God to be so displeased with me that His promises would no longer apply to me?

I know that might sound dramatic, but those thoughts were exacerbated every time other Christians reminded me of the only three words they knew about the death of a marriage: *God. Hates. Divorce.*

I (Joel) clearly remember one of my hardest ministry days. It was a day when my ministry life truly collided with my personal life. You see, I love what I get to do at Proverbs 31 Ministries as director of theology. What makes it even more special is that I get to process theology with people who aren't just coworkers but have truly become friends. We celebrate the highs and lows of life. We attend weddings, celebrate the birth of kids, and we also grieve the loss of parents and, yes, even the death of a marriage.

On this day, I was at Lysa's house sitting with another coworker and friend, Leah. We had a study day planned and deep theology to discuss. Leah and I were waiting at the gray round table for Lysa to join us. As she sat down, I noticed that her eyes were red and she had been crying. The tears had probably stopped flowing hours before, but the pain was still evident. This was a different kind of sorrow. I could feel the grief she was carrying on her shoulders. And we all felt the sobriety of that moment.

Then, Lysa looked at me and asked me one of the hardest questions I've ever had to respond to. The difficulty of it wasn't just the theology behind the question but the real-life implications of what the answer would mean.

Lysa asked, "Joel, is it true that God hates divorce?"

I imagine you may have asked this before too.

The simple fact that you are courageously asking this question is evidence that you want to honor God. You want to make Jesus proud. You want to do the right thing, and no part of you wants to get this wrong. The thought of dishonoring God through divorce probably feels debilitating.

No matter what stage you are in in this journey—pre-divorce, pending divorce, or post-divorce—I'd love to help bring some clarity to this big question. When you hear the statement "God hates divorce," you may think that, unfortunately, regardless of any situation and circumstance, if you get a divorce, you are facing not just the displeasure of God but the hatred of God. But where did this idea come from? Malachi 2:16.

Here's the challenge: The Hebrew in Malachi 2:16, the original language this book of the Bible was written in, makes it one of the most difficult verses to translate. That's why so many different Bible translations say different things in this verse. I honestly think this may be one of the more important Bible teachings that we desperately need to get right because of the devastation that takes place when we get it wrong. So we are going to do some deeper Bible study here. It will be worth it.

A quick history lesson on Bible translations will help us understand how we got to the phrase "God hates divorce." Today, we have a variety of translations of the Bible. Some people use NIV, others use ESV, and I personally study from CSB. But before all this variety, the primary translation people used was the King James Version of the Bible (KJV), specifically King James Version 1611, which was later updated to the New King James Version (NKJV). This was one of the first widely produced and distributed English Bibles, and it made a huge impact on our interpretation of the text because future translations would look to the KJV and NKJV as a starting point.

Ultimately, the translators of the KJV and NKJV made an interpretation decision instead of just leaving it at what the text says.[1] And I think KJV and NKJV got Malachi 2:16 terribly wrong. Let's look at the NKJV:

> "The LORD God of Israel says that *He hates divorce*, for it covers one's garment with violence," says the LORD of hosts. "Therefore take heed to your spirit, that you do not deal treacherously." (NKJV)

Why did the KJV/NKJV opt for "God hates divorce"? I'm honestly not sure. My suspicion is that, at some level, the translation decision was somehow influenced by a fear of promoting divorce. Regardless of the possible motivation, we have ancient manuscripts and original-language analysis that can help us find some clarity on what the original Hebrew was trying to convey. I'm going to summarize this here for you. But for my deeper Bible study gals and ministry-leader friends, follow the endnote for a more technical discussion.[2]

When making translation decisions, we want to follow the most ancient sources, as well as the history of interpretation. Admittedly, the Hebrew of Malachi 2:16 is incredibly difficult. When you translate one language into another, there is often not a one-to-one equivalent for the words you're translating. So all translations have to adjust the original Hebrew in order to make grammatical sense in English. When the Hebrew is adjusted, we may come up with a phrase like "God hates divorce," but this isn't the only way to read the original Hebrew. There is another way we can interpret the Hebrew to work in English, and I would suggest this is the more accurate reading. When we keep the Hebrew intact (following with ancient sources), we would translate the verb "he hates" as third person. The "he" in this instance is actually the husband, not God.

Let's look at how modern translations like the CSB and ESV handle this:

> "If he [*the husband*] hates and divorces his wife," says the LORD God of Israel, "he [*the husband*] covers his garment with injustice," says the LORD of Armies. Therefore, watch yourselves carefully, and do not act treacherously. (CSB)

> "*The man who does not love his wife but divorces her*," says the LORD, the God of Israel, "covers his garment with violence," says the LORD of hosts. So guard yourselves in your spirit, and do not be faithless." (ESV)

Finally, look at the distinction the NIV makes in response to the action:

> "*The man who hates and divorces his wife*," says the LORD, the God of Israel, "*does violence to the one he should protect*," says the LORD Almighty. So be on your guard, and do not be unfaithful. (NIV)

Simply put, the husband is the one doing the hating in this verse. The phrase "he covers his garments with injustice/violence" refers to the man being "unjust" and "cruel" toward his wife rather than protecting her. And Yahweh (God) is talking about His anger toward the husband, who is the one who has broken covenant.

Now, hear me say this loud and clear: God does hate what divorce does to people, families, and the individuals who are walking through it. Let's take a closer look at the Hebrew verb *śānēʾ* that is used in this verse. It is best and most accurately translated in English as "hate" and has the underlying meaning of "an emotional condition of aversion."[3] Other words we could also use are "scorn, grief, or even a change in status to being an enemy."[4] All these words are trying to get us to a deep sense of aversion toward the breaking of covenant and the impact it has on the innocent party. The last portion of the verse in Malachi 2:16 says, "Therefore, watch yourselves carefully, and do not act treacherously" (CSB). When we read the "therefore," we now shift to God's perspective on the situation and can make two observations: (1) the warning about how we must watch ourselves and be careful, and (2) how He views the situation of hatred toward an innocent spouse as treacherous. Ultimately, God is displeased with the one who unjustly breaks the marriage covenant they made with their spouse.

Now, keep in mind that God also forgives, redeems, and restores the repentant of heart. There is an overwhelming number of Scripture references that speak to this amazing truth about our gracious God. We truly can begin to comprehend the extravagance of the grace of God only when we come to terms with the tragedy of our sin. But if the offending party isn't repentant and breaks the covenant unjustly, he does violence to the one he should protect, as Malachi states, and God is displeased.

Let me be clear. With all our studying and reframing of this verse, I am not giving a license for divorce. I am not demeaning or lowering the sacred nature of marriage. I am not denying marriage is a covenant (*berith*) between a man and a woman in the presence of God as a judge. What I am saying is that this verse does not say "God hates divorce." The Hebrew doesn't read that way. The ancient sources don't read that way. And this distinction makes a difference! It matters. Why? Because, as Jim says, "The words we use frame the world we live in."

The translation "God hates divorce" is a flat and absolute statement. It is one that places God's hatred, grief, and displeasure equally on both the covenant breaker and the victim of the broken covenant. For the woman who is the recipient of an unwanted divorce, when she hears "God hates divorce," she hears "God hates what I am doing" or, worse, "God hates me." You may say that I am making an assumption about the heartbreaking misapplication of this verse. Let me assure you, this is not an assumption. I've personally heard the testimony of hundreds of women who have said that this verse was used to force them to stay in sexually, physically, and emotionally abusive marriages. When you add in the online comments, messages, and emails, the number of stories skyrockets into the thousands. This painful misplacement of God's displeasure is exactly that, a misplacement.

You see, there are biblical reasons that make a divorce possible and even necessary (more on that in the next chapter). Does it break God's heart? Of course. Is it ideal? No, of course not. But at times, in some situations, it's not only permissible but necessary. Shame comes from the Enemy and is never from God. So as Christians, we need to be careful of misunderstanding a verse and then misapplying it to people, causing them shame or, worse, forcing them to stay in what our friend Leslie Vernick calls a destructive marriage.

This is why clarity on what this verse is actually saying matters. It protects innocent victims of unwanted divorces and those who have been rescued from marriages that threaten their well-being from feeling like they are in sin and are a disappointment to God. They are not. In fact, the entire concept of the Old Testament certificate of divorce was established to protect women.

Some people have responded to this idea and said that moving away from the phrase "God hates divorce" is a dangerous thing because it devalues the covenant of marriage. But this is a comment based on fear, and fear as a motivation makes for horrible hermeneutics (how we study and interpret the Bible). The truth is, this passage, translated appropriately, maintains the right view of marriage. This helps us see that the grief and displeasure of God are directed toward the one who breaks the covenant. With this insight, we can see the tragic effect that this covenant-breaking action has upon the innocent victim. We can see the devastation that occurs when the sacredness of marriage is shattered, while simultaneously tending to the heart of the victim who was sinned against. None of this devalues or diminishes the institution of marriage. It upholds it in the proper order.

The entire concept of the Old Testament certificate of divorce was established to protect women.

What grieves me the most is that some in the church put undue suffering on the women who have been crushed by the sinful choices of men who are in the throes of sin (cheating, abusing, exploiting), being more concerned about the woman potentially getting a divorce than about addressing the reasons the woman is in this position in the first place. The comments that have grieved me the most are the ones from Christian ministry leaders who haven't said a word about the sin, betrayals, deceitfulness, and unrepentant nature of the men who are breaking the hearts of women by the millions. This is why accurate and faithful exegesis is paramount. This is why having compassionate hearts is essential. This is why humble theology matters.

So for the sister who wanted nothing more than to please God with her life, who now has the word *divorced* attached to her circumstances, let me say this to you: God does not hate you. He is not displeased with you. He loves you, cherishes you, and is so proud of your courage as you walk through something you never created, never wanted, but are now facing.

I (Lysa) want you to have this insight because it truly comforted me and equipped me with the truth I needed so I wouldn't have to add the fear of getting it wrong biblically on top of my relational heartbreak. But I don't want you to feel like we are sitting in a cold, stark classroom rather than the comforts of my living room. So as we close this chapter, I want you to do three things:

- Listen to the song "Thank God I Do" by Lauren Daigle. Close your eyes and let the beautiful words and melody wash over you.

- Go outside, stand in the grass, and look up at the sky. It's still there. Even though your world feels like it is falling apart at times, the world is still traveling around the sun. It's still on its axis, and the sky is not falling down around you. Find something in God's beautiful creation to help you remember He is not absent. His beauty still exists in the world. And your story is not finished.
- Call a friend who needs the truths from this chapter. When we take the comfort we have received and share it with others, this is a step toward healing.

Also, for those whose reasons for divorce included infidelity, it can feel a little more clear-cut, but for others it can feel much murkier. While none of us should look for an excuse for divorce, in the next chapter Joel is going to walk you through an in-depth view of what the Bible does say and does not say about biblical grounds for divorce.

COUNSELOR'S CORNER WITH JIM

Shame can be driven by so many things: "Being divorced was never part of my plan." "*Divorce* is not even in my vocabulary!" "How can my ex move on as though our marriage had never existed?" "How in the world could he already be in another romantic relationship?" Or, even worse, "How could he already be on the runway to marry another woman?"

Sadly, shame is often the evil companion of divorced people. I describe shame primarily as Self-Hatred-At-My-Expense.

I also spell shame as Social-Hatred-At-My-Expense and Satanic-Hatred-At-My-Expense.

So often, individuals who have experienced an unwanted divorce will face their own internal condemnation (self-hatred). This can be exacerbated by their ex-spouse's statements, like "We were in a loveless marriage" or "We just got married too young." If that's true, fine. But if that's not true, he may be rewriting history to confuse you, controlling the narrative to justify his bad behavior, and making you doubt what really happened. So many women feel shame and emotional vertigo when a spouse does this, and they turn it inward and shame themselves unnecessarily. Shame can also come about through condemnation from the world, including family, friends, other Christians, and Christian leaders (social hatred). And shame can come from the toxic condemnation of Satan and his evil forces (satanic hatred).

Now, shame does have a neurobiological payoff. Shame is often an attempt to numb out pain. I have often pinched my hand when I am getting my blood drawn or receiving a shot, because inflicting some pain in my hand will distract me from the pain of the needle. We do the same thing with shame. It's not always conscious; a lot of times it's subconscious. If we beat ourselves up in shame—"You're such a loser"—and then someone else comes along and calls us a loser, it doesn't hurt as bad. But one problem with the pinch of shame is we cannot pick and choose which emotions we numb. In her research around shame, Brené Brown found that "we cannot selectively numb emotions.

When we numb the painful emotions, we also numb the positive emotions."[5] We end up not just numbing the pain but numbing everything else too.

It is vital that you take counsel with yourself (Nehemiah 5:7 ESV) when shame bubbles up, that you respond to it with biblical truth, love, and healthy thinking. We will continue to help you with this throughout the book, but I invite you to begin taking control of your thoughts of shame now as a regular, daily practice. In doing this, you will be sitting in the place of a wise, biblically informed counselor to yourself.

Today forward, led by Jesus Christ, you are the landlord of your mind and life, and it is time for some evictions! Remember Romans 8:1: "There is therefore now no condemnation for those who are in Christ Jesus" (ESV).

CHAPTER 4

Is the Only Valid Reason for Divorce Sexual Infidelity?

You know what's really hard to swallow? I've (Lysa) actually had to admit that, as awful as it was in 2016 discovering that my spouse cheated on me, in the end at least it made my divorce a little more acceptable to some people. I get it on the one hand, because it makes things a little more definitive. But on the other hand, is that really what Scripture says? That sexual infidelity is the only biblical reason for divorce? Again, I in no way want to teach something that isn't biblically accurate. And it's because of the confusion around this that Joel and I wrote this chapter.

For so many women, this teaching about divorce has caused such anguish because infidelity wasn't part of their destructive relationship. Or they couldn't prove that infidelity played a part in their marriage. But other forms of abuse and neglect happened that are definitely not part of God's design for marriage, nor are they things a woman should have to just suffer through.

One of my friends who was in this situation for years endured verbal and sexual abuse that almost broke her. She desperately didn't want to dishonor God. But the severity of what she was experiencing was no longer something she could withstand. After years of working with her counselors, separating and getting back together, watching the promises he made to change get broken time after time, and seeking the Lord's direction through prayer and biblical counseling, she took the excruciating step to finally say *no more*. Her husband hadn't cheated, and due to the nature of the abuse she endured, she kept details private. But since the whole story wasn't shared, people misunderstood. She even got a text from a Christian friend who heard about the divorce and sent three horrible words: SHAME ON YOU.

Good grief.

When my friend told me this, I dropped my head and wanted to weep. Let's just take a deep breath and stand in agreement that we all hate what divorce does to people. Yes. But then we need to get a little more educated on what the Bible actually says are the biblical grounds for this excruciating decision.

In my (Joel) experience, it's pretty common for people to say that sexual infidelity is the only valid biblical reason for divorce. Sadly, this rationale has been used to encourage women in emotionally destructive and physically unsafe marriages to stay in their situations, because "he didn't have an affair." Verses in the New Testament that are used to weaponize this position, however, are taken out of context, and the people using them in this way often lack the required Old Testament knowledge for properly understanding New Testament verses in the overarching framework of the Bible. To counter that, it's important for us to spend some time digging into what the Bible actually does say about the possibility of a divorce. *This is not intended to be a loophole to get you out of an uncomfortable marriage.* My hope is to give you the best biblical context possible so you can have a larger perspective to make the most informed, God-honoring, and self-dignifying decision.

One of the things I often say to Lysa and the team at Proverbs 31 Ministries is that there are things in the Bible that are not intended to be policies but, rather, are meant to be understood as principles. This chapter is designed to expound on the larger principles that God has revealed to us in His Word for the tragic scenario where there is the death of a marriage. So, friend, take these principles and process them with trusted friends. Submit them to the Holy Spirit. Bring them into the wise counsel of pastors and a therapist. And, in the end, just do the best you can with what you have and continue to put your trust in Jesus along the way.

So what does the Bible say about the valid reasons for a divorce? It is true that most of the time the reason for a valid divorce is isolated to sexual infidelity. This comes from Matthew 19:7–9:

> "Why then," they asked him, "did *Moses command* us to give divorce papers and to send her away?" He told them, "*Moses permitted* you to divorce your wives because of the hardness of your hearts, but it was not like that from the beginning. I tell you, whoever divorces his wife, except for sexual immorality, and marries another commits adultery." (CSB)

At a surface reading, it may seem like Jesus allows divorce only in the case of sexual immorality. But we have to remember that Jesus was speaking in a very specific cultural context. So when He made this statement, the original audience would have mentally included other details from their background knowledge. In this instance, they would have been like, "Oh, yeah, and of course we would include Deuteronomy 24:1–4 as the other two valid reasons for divorce." Because that audience would have naturally added this in, He wouldn't need to explicitly say it.

Is this already starting to feel complicated, with all the subtext and cultural context? Before we get into deep Bible study with Deuteronomy, more unpacking of this passage in Matthew, and how Paul understood this in his writings, let me give you a little encouragement. You actually do a great job with culture and context already!

Here's a very practical, right-now example: Lysa lives part-time near Jacksonville, Florida, where there are many NFL Jaguars fans. Imagine Lysa calling and saying, "It's such a bummer that the Jags had a losing season." How would you respond? You might say something like, "That stinks, but honestly I can't really relate because we aren't a football family." Or "I feel your pain. We've been waiting for our team to have a winning season for a long time."

But wait, how did you know we were talking about football? And how did you know that the "Jags" didn't mean an animal called a jaguar or a really nice luxury car? What connected all the dots for you? Cultural, social, and historical context!

Let me encourage you. You do this all the time, even without putting much thought into it. You are so familiar with the current context of the world you live in that, for the most part, you don't have to work too hard to understand the intention and meaning of what people say to you. Now we just need to learn the context of the Old and New Testaments, so you can apply it to the biblical text.

Let's look at Deuteronomy 24:1–4:

> "If a man marries a woman, but she becomes displeasing to him because he finds something *indecent* [*ervat davar*] about her, he may write her a divorce certificate, hand it to her, and send her away from his house. If after leaving his house she goes and becomes another man's wife, and the second man *hates* [*shana*] her, writes her a divorce certificate, hands it to her, and sends her away from his house or if he dies, the first husband who sent her away may not marry her again after she has been defiled, because that would be detestable to the LORD. You must not bring guilt on the land the LORD your God is giving you as an inheritance." (CSB)

We must consider two Hebrew phrases here: the terms *ervat davar* (indecent) and *shana* (hatred). The Hebrew for "indecent" (*ervat davar*) is notoriously difficult to translate. Old Testament scholars are divided on this. Some view this as a reference to adultery, some kind of physical abnormality, or simply something displeasing. It seems to me the issue cannot be adultery, because the consequence for that was clearly stated as death (Deuteronomy 22:22). So it may be the issue is some kind of impurity dealing with the inability to have children.[1]

We need to be careful that we don't impose our twenty-first-century understanding into this text. Let's fight hard to understand the verse in its natural context. I know you are probably wondering why this kind of exception would be acceptable and how that would impact the woman unable to have children. The society during this time was heavily dependent on children to continue family legacy and also the household vocation. This permittance of divorce due to an inability to have children probably has to do with that and was not necessarily a reference to the worth or dignity of the woman.

Now let's look at the second phrase. The Hebrew for "hatred" (*shana*), as seen in the context of Hosea 9:15 and what we covered earlier in Malachi 2:16, is understood as a technical term for divorce.[2] We can gather from this evidence that the ancient Israelites had a view that divorce was permissible under certain situations. This was never the ideal, but the care and support of victims of unwanted divorces was of utmost importance to God.

Please don't miss this. *The care and support of victims of unwanted divorces was of utmost importance to God.*

The whole rationale for a certificate of divorce was to ensure the woman had the opportunity to remarry and survive in a patriarchal society. This was unique to the Israelites, as the concept of a divorce certificate was otherwise unknown in the Ancient Near Eastern world (the context of the Old Testament).[3]

I want us to pause at this point. The known world at the time did not have a legitimate way for a woman in an abusive situation to seek a way out of that situation. God cares so much for women and victims of unwanted divorce that He put a policy in place for their protection.

When is divorce biblically acceptable? Part of how we know what verses meant and how they were interpreted is through the witness of the early teachers of the Bible. Within the context of Jewish community, these "teachers of the law" were called "rabbis." The rabbis understood that three major areas constituted a valid rationale for divorce. They got this, in part, from Exodus 21:10–11, which required the husband to provide "food, clothing, [and] marital rights."

> If he takes an additional wife, he must not reduce the food, clothing, or marital rights of the first wife. And if he does not do these three things for her, she may leave free of charge, without any payment. (CSB)

We could summarize these three categories under the umbrella of neglect. The husband could become guilty of abandoning his wife in the case of material neglect, emotional neglect, and physical neglect.

- Material neglect: withholding food, clothing, or shelter
- Emotional neglect: withholding conjugal rights, though the rabbis also had in mind a type of cruelty and humiliation
- Physical neglect: unfaithfulness, adultery, and physical abuse

The rabbis had a system to protect women, and one of the ways they did this was by creating a process where women could present proof of material neglect, emotional neglect, or physical neglect. Since the rabbis had already done what they could to get the husband to stop his neglectful or destructive behaviors by this point (their first action would have been to levy a fine on the offending party, in hopes of helping the couple return to the ideal of marriage as established by God), they then turned their attention to rescuing the woman out of that environment. At this point, the rabbis would put pressure on the man to give the woman a certificate of divorce. This was the only way for the woman to have the opportunity to remarry. If the man refused to release his wife from having to endure the cruel circumstances within the marriage, the *Mishnah* (a Jewish collection of oral tradition, a foundational framework of Judaism) details an additional financial penalty that would have been placed on the man. In some extreme cases, the rabbis were forced to revert to physical punishment and the man was whipped.[4]

Okay, let's have a moment of honesty here. Maybe you are nodding your head in agreement. Heck, you may even be screaming amen and hallelujah at the thought of this situation being applied to yours! Now, I am not in any way condoning what these rabbinic commentators suggest. But I do think it's important for you to see that a tradition of interpretation was in place to protect the rights of the woman who was the victim of an unwanted divorce due to abandonment through any of these three categories of neglect.

If a woman succeeded in showing a valid rationale for a divorce, she was granted the divorce certificate and also kept the dowry (*ketubah*) and any penalties or fines the husband had paid. This is another important detail. This shows that God wanted the woman to be free and safe and also set up for success in her future endeavors without the covering of her husband.

Okay, but what about what the New Testament says?

As we explore some of the most direct statements from Jesus on divorce, I want us to recall how we started this section about the importance of the social, historical, and cultural context of the Bible. When Jesus spoke, He did so with this context in mind.

This means we should be reading His statements and considering how those original hearers and readers of these words would fill in some of the contextual clues that framed what He was saying.

Back to Matthew 19. Jesus was cornered by some Pharisees, who began to drill him on divorce. There is a reason they asked these specific questions. They were trying to trap Jesus. They wanted to get Jesus into a well-known and fiercely debated argument regarding the correct interpretation of the word for "indecency" (*ervat davar*) and if it implies just *any* indecency or a *specific* indecency (Deuteronomy 24:1–4). The Pharisees wanted to pin Jesus in either the Hillel or Shammai camp (or school of thought).

The Hillel school of thought recognized that the Hebrew phrase *ervat davar* could refer to either "a matter" or "an indecency." So they came up with an understanding that, for "any matter of indecency," a divorce could take place. One extreme example found in rabbinic writings is that a husband could get a divorce if his wife "spoiled a dish."[5] As you can imagine, there are issues here! The Shammai school of thought, on the other hand, viewed divorce as viable only as a result of indecency as displayed in adultery.

Jesus recognized the trap laid out in front of Him. He realized the Pharisees wanted him to make a choice between these two major schools of thought, Hillel or Shammai, and He masterfully dismantled the trap.

"Some Pharisees approached him to test him. They asked, 'Is it lawful for a man to divorce his wife on any grounds?'" (Matthew 19:3 CSB). But Jesus started the discussion about marriage and divorce with a side tangent, which was intentional. He started by saying, "Haven't you read?" which I personally think is an epic Jesus comeback moment. The Pharisees were supposed to be known for their vast reading, and Jesus questioned them on this very basis! He first went to God's ideal for marriage as being between one man and one woman. Therefore, the concept of marriage was intended to be monogamous, not polygamous. This was an important clarifier, because in the ancient world, polygamy was acceptable (though was slowly going out of favor among the Israelites). In this type of polygamous society, adultery was always an offense against the husband. It referred to the sexual unfaithfulness of a married woman. A man could have sex with an unmarried woman and, in doing so, technically did not commit adultery but fornication.

Jesus wouldn't stand for this. The implication in his reply is a widening of the context of adultery, meaning that if a man sleeps with someone other than his wife, it is adultery in the same way as if a woman commits sexual infidelity against her husband. In other words, before Jesus even got into the question of divorce, He intentionally elevated the value and worth of women.

Let's look at how the conversation unfolded in Matthew 19:7–9:

> "Why then," they asked him, "did *Moses command* us to give divorce papers and to send her away?" He told them, "*Moses permitted* you to divorce your wives because of the hardness of your hearts, but it was not like that from the beginning. I tell you, whoever divorces his wife, except for sexual immorality, and marries another commits adultery." (CSB)

The Pharisees were quoting from and interpreting Deuteronomy 24:1, which says, "He may write her a divorce certificate, hand it to her, and send her away from his house" (CSB). The Hebrew grammar here, when it says "he may," is neutral. It could be "he should" or "he may." The Pharisees went with the interpretation that it's more of a concrete command that "he must," but Jesus clarified and interpreted it through the lens of the gospel and said it is "he may" or "it is allowed but not demanded." Further, Jesus said the allowance of the divorce is based on "hardness of heart" or "human stubbornness." This means that Jesus left room for divorce in the case of the offender showing a "hardness of heart" through persistent, stubborn unrepentance.

Jesus intentionally elevated the value and worth of women.

Jesus was saying that the Hillel understanding of "any matter," commonly known as "for any reason" divorce, is inconsistent with the way of God. Further, divorce in the context of adultery is allowed but not demanded.

Let's go back to the issue of culture and context. Some people would interpret this to mean that adultery is the only acceptable reason for divorce. But remember, Jesus was pulling from the story of Israel in the Old Testament. He was intentionally referring to the place in Scripture that touches on the issue of neglect (emotional, material, physical). The original hearer would *not* have heard this as saying divorce is restricted only to cases of adultery. They would have filled in the gaps and recognized Jesus, of course, had in mind the other categories or "valid grounds."

I appreciate how Dr. Instone-Brewer, one of the leading scholars on the study of divorce in the Bible, put it:

> Contemporary Jews would have mentally added something like this exception, whether it was present or not. They would either have added "except for valid grounds" (if they were thinking of divorce in general) or "except for indecency" (if they were thinking just about Deuteronomy 24:1).[6]

Another "problem passage," or at least one that can be confusing, is Paul's discussion of marriage, divorce, and remarriage in 1 Corinthians 7.

First, we need to understand the Greco-Roman world during Paul's time. People in this society had total freedom to get a divorce, which created an environment where marriage wasn't taken seriously. This reflects the Hillel school of thought, where separation and dismissal of a marriage union could happen for any reason. A marriage contract was written almost like the modern-day will. If divorce occurred, the contract identified who received what financial provisions and assets. This created an ethical dilemma. If you wanted out of your marriage because you wanted money and resources for yourself, you could just start the divorce proceeding and get out of the marriage. The point is, it wasn't difficult. Further, in the Greco-Roman context, men and women could divorce each other for any reason. The owner of the house could tell their partner to leave. Or the partner could just move out and, at that point, they were considered as good as divorced. Okay, now with all this background information, we can make sense of what Paul was saying in 1 Corinthians 7.

In this passage, it seems Paul was speaking to this specific cultural and social issue. He wanted to correct the pendulum swing and draw us back to the obligations of covenant marriage, rooted in the Old Testament passages we looked at. Of course, adultery or unfaithfulness was a given as a valid reason for divorce. But Paul went back to the Old Testament understanding and also dealt with the emotional obligations of marriage in

1 Corinthians 7:1–5 and the material obligations of marriage in 1 Corinthians 7:32–35. He rejected the Greco-Roman version of the Hillel divorce through separation for any reason but left an allowance for "valid" divorce based on unfaithfulness, emotional neglect, or material neglect.

The key challenge for us as we study what the Bible says about divorce is not to fall into the trap of the Hillel view and opt out of a marriage simply because it has become uncomfortable, inconvenient, or just too hard. There is a difference between someone acting out of selfishness and someone who leaves selfishness unattended so it eventually becomes self-destruction. This is why having wise counsel, relying on the direction and leading of the Holy Spirit, and seeking out professional counseling and therapeutic help is so important.

We've covered a lot of biblical ground in this chapter. As a theologian, I find that researching and writing on topics and questions like these feels weighty. It's so important to me to emphasize that I am not here to justify divorce. I don't want these words to be misunderstood or misrepresented. But I also don't want people to suffer because they've been misinformed. My deepest desire is to help you know the truth, because "the truth will set you free" (John 8:32 CSB). God's Word should not be weaponized against us or used to bully or shame us. It should be used to lead us closer to Him, convict us of our sin, and ultimately lead us to freedom. And that freedom should lead to further healing.

Psalm 107:20 says, "He sent his word and healed them; he rescued them from their traps" (CSB). Remember these words, my friend. Resist the temptation to turn away from the Lord when you have questions and deep wrestling in your soul. Instead, allow God's Word to pull you into further freedom and healing.

COUNSELOR'S CORNER WITH JIM

Outside of Scripture, this quote by Scott Peck in *The Road Less Traveled* is my most-cited statement over the past twenty-five years of counseling work I've done: "Mental health is an ongoing process of dedication to reality at all costs."[7] When I say this to my clients, I usually state it this way: "Mental health is a commitment to reality at all costs." Please stop and read that again, specifically the end. "At all costs." In all my years of counseling, I have never told someone to get a divorce. What I have done is walk alongside people as they have come to their own conclusions and equip them with their own therapeutic wisdom to process one of the hardest decisions of their lives.

Whether you are still trying to decide what to do or are currently divorced, or even remarried, I want to give you a tool to continue to "[speak] the truth in love" (Ephesians 4:15 CSB) to yourself, helping you stay committed to reality at all costs.

Get a sheet of paper and make two columns. At the top of one column, write "Facts of What I've Experienced in My Marriage." This could include anything your spouse has done or said that has hurt you. Label the second column "The Impact of What These Facts Have Done to Me." Consider the impacts on your mind, your mental, physical, emotional, and spiritual health, your finances, and simply the impact on your one precious life you are privileged to live on this earth.

When Lysa was in one of the hardest seasons of trying to save her marriage but continually experiencing new traumas, her colon twisted. She had to have surgery to save her life. The surgeon asked Lysa if she had been in a serious car wreck because the trauma inside her body was so significant. She had not been in a physical accident. She was experiencing significant emotional trauma. Afterward, she brought me a picture the doctor had given her. In all my years of counseling, I had never seen an actual picture of the cost of ongoing emotional trauma inside the body. Since that day, I've never been able to let go of that realization. So when I say to count the cost to your health, I want you to be very honest about the toll your experience is taking on you.

If your divorce was years ago, I still want you to examine the ramifications of what you walked through. And if you have children, certainly consider the impact of a toxic, destructive, or unhealthy marriage on them. I will often say to women who come to see me, "Your kids deserve one healthy parent." Doing these exercises and taking an honest look at how this experience has affected you can be an important part of your healing.

If you are doing this exercise by yourself and you get activated or flooded with emotion or memories, find a trusted friend or a counselor to help you process these realities. What we are doing here is counting the true cost, which is how you've been affected. If we don't examine how you've been impacted, you can't possibly experience all the healing you need.

CHAPTER 5

Why Hasn't God Stopped All This from Happening?

When you're in the throes of divorce, even if you feel firmly planted in what the Bible says about it, sometimes the suffering can still feel incredibly intense. It can seem like God is not intervening on your behalf. For me (Lysa), doubting that God was with me wasn't the issue. What broke my heart over and over was the fact that I deeply believed God loved me, cared for me, and was all powerful, and yet in some situations it felt like He was doing nothing to help me. I remember writing in my journal over and over, *God sees me, God knows what's happening, and He is in the process of delivering me.* But after writing these statements with confidence, I felt increasingly confused. I was writing what I felt I should say but not what I really felt.

Hard things kept happening. The tide seemed to be going in the direction of my ex-husband. So many times, it appeared as if he was living his best life while at the same time things were getting harder and harder for me. He had found another woman right away. He was taking dream vacations. He wasn't involved with the kids' emotional fallout. He didn't have the weight of trying to keep things the same for the kids, along with the added financial pressure of going from a two-income household to one.

Where was the justice in all this? Where was my rescue? Where was some sort of reprieve for me?

I had tried so hard to honor God and do the right things. I knew I wasn't perfect, but in my heart I had this nagging sense that I had done what God required of me, so where was that big moment when He stopped more hard things from happening to me?

My divorce was almost settled. But the attacks were not.

My ex-husband filed claims against me in a lawsuit. As I read his allegations, my mouth fell open and my heart started pounding in my chest. I just kept saying over and over, "This can't be real. I can't keep doing this. Why in the world would God allow this?" Once again, my world turned upside down and any feeling of stability I'd started to gain splintered apart. What I had to do to defend myself against his accusations hijacked my schedule, my emotions, and any assurance I had that I would eventually be okay. Not to mention the money it cost.

The legal deposition was so hard. I had to answer questions meant to trip me up, make me look bad, and accuse me of really hurtful things. I remember sitting in that chair, feeling like my head was going to explode because of all that was being done to make me look like the bad guy. In the end, I was able to prevail, but regardless, the things said about me that day left their mark.

Then, before I could get through that lawsuit, he filed another lawsuit.

When would this madness ever stop?

For some, divorce can be amicable. But for many women it's

not. When you are locked in a bitter battle with vastly different narratives and opinions about what should happen, divorce is not just the signing of a few papers, the separation of belongings, and decisions about custody of the kids. It's another whole wave of heartbreak.

I've often thought, *I am the mother of your children. If for no other reason, can you let that fact soften your heart toward me?*

And for those whose kids are young, I also want to recognize that it is so very painful to hand your children over to the other parent when, in essence, that person is now your opponent in court. And it can be even harder if he's already found another woman who is now spending time with your kids. I remember one of my friends telling me about the first time she watched her kids being picked up by her ex for his weekend with them. His new girlfriend was in the car. As the four of them drove off, she felt like her life had been stolen. For the next few days, another woman would be living the life she was supposed to be living.

No one should ever have to experience that kind of pain. If that is you, I just want to pause right here and say I am so sorry. I don't want you to have to go another second without someone recognizing how much stress and strain is on you as the mom in this dynamic.

Just yesterday, I heard from two women who are each in the throes of divorce legal battles, where it very much seems like evil is winning. It's hard to get a true gauge of that when you're in the middle of the battle, but when you have to hear the other attorney rip you to shreds, it sure seems like you've hit one of the worst lows there is. If that's where you are or what you've been through, I hate that you had to add this form of suffering on top of everything else.

I was the child of divorced parents, and I remember being too young to really understand what was happening to my mom. As an adult who understands things much more clearly now, I wish I had been gentler with her then and more grateful for all she did for my sister and me.

Our kids were older when the lawsuits were happening, so custody wasn't a battle I had to fight. But watching our kids get caught in the crossfire was still brutal. *How can this be where our family ended up? How can this be the reality that our kids now have to witness? And why does it have to last so long?* It all seemed so pointless and painful and ridiculously costly.

I had hoped and hoped and hoped that I would see God turn things my way. But then one day I picked up my journal and realized I could no longer write about the faithfulness of God. I put my pen down and wept. *Why isn't God stopping this? Why is He allowing this to continue?*

Trying to answer these questions and hoping God would do what I assumed a good God should do was a dead end. No human could possibly explain this to me, because no human can fully understand the mind of God.

Maybe you are asking questions of your own today. I'm not going to attempt to give you a pat answer and spiritually tie this up neater than it ever will be. Even now, I still don't have answers to many of the questions I asked God. I want us to table what we don't know so we can be more productive with what we can know.

Two practices have helped me tremendously:

- Tracing God's hand of faithfulness from my past
- Tracing God's faithfulness inside His Word

Let's start with the first practice. I call it "tracing God's hand of faithfulness." Joel calls it "a theology of remembrance." Sometimes memories are painful. But the kind of memories I'm talking about are the ones where you can now see how God was doing good when nothing felt good to you in the moment. Pick one instance, big or small, where you have a new perspective and can thank God for how He worked things out. One of the examples from my life is the timing of my breast cancer diagnosis.

In 2017, things were especially chaotic, and I was an emotional wreck. I had made another heartbreaking discovery and had to take some time off work to get my bearings. During that time, I decided to go do all the checkup appointments that I usually put off because of my busy schedule. One of those was a mammogram. I wasn't due to have my mammogram quite yet, but since I had the time, I did it early. After a series of tests, it turned out I had breast cancer. At the time, I was completely shocked that God would allow another hard thing on top of the emotional devastation I was already dealing with. But I can now see that because the doctors caught it so early, I was able to have a double mastectomy and today I am cancer-free.

So was my marriage falling apart again that summer the worst thing? It sure felt like it at the time. Or was my marriage falling apart what gave me the time to get a mammogram and an early diagnosis, thus saving my life?

I couldn't see it that day when I was sitting with the doctor, feeling shocked to hear the word *cancer*. But I absolutely now see how God's faithfulness played out. I could share other smaller examples, but the only way they can help me see God's faithfulness is if I pause and choose to remember them, think about them, and declare how good God was. If I can remember how good He was, I can more easily believe how good He is, even when I don't feel it. Whatever your example is of the Lord being faithful in the past, remember that same faithful God who was working in that past circumstance is now handling your present circumstances.

That same faithful God who was working in that past circumstance is now handling your present circumstances.

The reason this is such an important practice is that when we forget, we maximize what problems we're facing today while minimizing what God has already done. When I only focus on what is so terrible right now, I fill in the gaps and I assume evil is winning and God is doing nothing. I forget we live in a world where sin runs rampant—not forever, but certainly right now—and there are things God does or allows that will not make sense to me in this moment and may not feel good to me at all.[1]

When I look back at God's past faithfulness, yes, there are still things I don't understand, that don't feel good, that I am grieving, and that don't look like I hoped they would. But I remember He knows more than we know. And that sometimes we just have to leave room for the mystery of God and have faith in His power because He's proven Himself faithful before, and He will again. I want to position myself in the place where I can look back and say, "My God, look at what You have done! You were with me. You were working things together for good. I couldn't see it then, but I see it now!"

When I've been tempted to say, "Why does it appear God is not doing anything?" I should've actually said, "I do not serve a do-nothing God. He is doing something . . . I just can't see it *yet*." This doesn't lessen my pain but it does increase my faith just enough to get through the next day and then the next.

So if you're having a hard time facing each new day and it seems like God is doing nothing, I understand. Please know I still have to freshly apply this. Just this week, something else happened that has threatened to send me into another emotional tailspin.

Tracing God's faithfulness from the past doesn't fix our present hardships, but it does ground us and give us a little bit more strength for today and hope for our better future.

The second practice is to turn to God's Word, allowing His truth to be our stabilizing force rather than trying to find stability in the rising and falling of all the circumstances we're currently navigating. Instead of trying to wrap our minds around it all, we've got to dive into the best stability we have: (1) God's Word and (2) the Holy Spirit's reminders of God's Word.

A hard truth I have reminded myself of so many times is this: The moments when I want to pick up the Bible the least are the moments I need to pick up the Bible the most. So, I want to give you some truths right now, and I've asked Joel to help us better understand what each truth means for us.

Friend, I (Joel) hope that when the suffering gets intense, when the things happening right now make no sense and the questions about why God isn't intervening the way you've begged Him to are haunting you, you come back to these truths.

TRUTH TO TURN TO

I am sure of this, that he who started a good work in you will carry it on to completion until the day of Christ Jesus. (Philippians 1:6 CSB)

WHAT THIS TRUTH MEANS FOR US

Sometimes when we are in the very middle of suffering, we zero in on all that is going wrong. In this verse, Paul, who was in the throes of suffering in prison (v. 7), reminds us that God is good and His work in our lives is always good, even if what we are experiencing in the moment doesn't feel good. In a way, this is an echo of the garden of Eden. In the creation story, everything God created was followed with "It is good" (Genesis 1). It seems Paul picked up on this, reminding us not to lose sight of the good that God is working in us. And even if the things happening to you feel anything but good, remember that God can take the harm done to you and work it for an eventual good (for example, take the life of Joseph: Genesis 50:20).

We can deal honestly with all the feelings that come with suffering, but we can also cling to the truth that God is not in the business of leaving us in a place of ruin. Our journey may go in directions we don't want it to go, and our suffering may not turn into comfort on this side of eternity, but let's remember that the good is actually in what He is developing inside us, regardless of the situations and the circumstances.

TRUTH TO TURN TO

Take up the full armor of God, so that you may be able to resist in the evil day, and having prepared everything, to take your stand. Stand, therefore, with truth like a belt around your waist, righteousness like armor on your chest, and your feet sandaled with readiness for the gospel of peace. (Ephesians 6:13–15 CSB)

WHAT THIS TRUTH MEANS FOR US

When we are suffering, it's easy to feel like we're alone. But God hasn't left us to fight a single battle by ourselves. Furthermore, Ephesians 6 tells us how we are to fight.

You may have heard a lot of sermons on the armor of God. One of the most important aspects of the armor is the focus on truth. Right away, we are told to fasten the belt of truth around our waist.

A fascinating detail about the armor of the Roman soldiers is that the belt had two functions. First, it established military rank and often put on display military heroics during battle (think about the medals soldiers get). Second, the belt carried the sword, the primary offensive weapon of the soldier and in some cases additionally a dagger running across the belt strap on the right or left shoulder.[2] Therefore, the belt is crucial as an indicator of who we belong to, and what we stand for. It is central to the believer because truth is the very center of the gospel (Ephesians 4:25).[3] Truth is what stabilizes us as we fight through suffering and hardship. We need truth fastened onto us so we can separate what is true and what is false. Even more, in wisdom, we can determine what is true and what is almost true. Truth equips us to discern, and discernment is crucial for our fight.

TRUTH TO TURN TO

My heart shudders within me; terrors of death sweep over me. Fear and trembling grip me; horror has overwhelmed me. I said, "If only I had wings like a dove! I would fly away and find rest." . . . But I call to God, and the Lord will save me. (Psalm 55:4–6, 16 CSB)

WHAT THIS TRUTH MEANS FOR US

When we are suffering, we want the suffering to end. Which is not only understandable, but totally normal.

But there may be something we need to do first. We need to deal with the fear that often fuels our suffering. David understood this so well. He talked about the terror, fear, and trembling that had a grip on him (Psalm 55). The outcome of these fears is suffering. And the worst part of fear is that it has a way of keeping us frozen in the suffering. Now that we understand that, what do we do about it?

First, we have to be honest and name our fears for what they are. David identified his fears as coming from the words of his enemies, from the sinking feeling of others acting in wicked ways toward him, and from the disaster and harassment that came from those determined to do him harm (Psalm 55:3). Even worse, David said some of this was coming from people he thought were his friends. I have a suspicion we may all be raising our hands, nodding our heads, saying, "Totally get it." So how did David handle this? How are we supposed to handle this? David said, "But I call to God, and the Lord will save me" (v. 16).

Here are a few more assurances that may bring you comfort and courage that are also found in Psalm 55: "God, the one enthroned from long ago, will hear and will humiliate them *Selah* because they do not change and do not fear God" (v. 22 CSB). Notice the selah, a musical note intentionally placed in the middle of this verse. This is God's Word directing us to pause on this, think about it, and believe it is true. We should factor this in when we fear those who just keep hurting us over and over. If they have humiliated us without repenting, they will themselves eventually be humiliated. This is where Lysa would say, "And all my justice girls said, 'Amen!'"

Then, toward the end of the psalm, David encouraged us to "cast your burden on the LORD, and he will sustain you; he will never allow the righteous to be shaken" (v. 22 CSB). Notice the word *shaken* in this verse. Will there be times things feel imbalanced? Yes. But the Word of God is our anchor that we can turn to over and over to regain our stability and hope.

TRUTH TO TURN TO

I am persuaded that neither death nor life, nor angels nor rulers, nor things present nor things to come, nor powers, nor height nor depth, nor any other created thing will be able to separate us from the love of God that is in Christ Jesus our Lord. (Romans 8:38–39 CSB)

WHAT THIS TRUTH MEANS FOR US

Certain things take place that we won't ever understand on this side of eternity. And, honestly, that is just tough to come to terms with. But we need to work toward an acceptance of this perspective. One way we can do this is to remember that, regardless of the why of suffering, we can be confident of the *who* that is with us in the midst of that suffering.[4] Even more assuring is that nothing can separate us from Him. This can be easy to forget when we're consumed with the pain from someone who vowed to love us, cherish us, and be by our side but has now left us. So hold on to this truth today: Jesus will never lose His grip on us, even when we feel like we are losing our grip on everything else. We are safely held in the faithful hands of Christ.

TRUTH TO TURN TO

We also boast in our afflictions, because we know that affliction produces endurance, endurance produces proven character, and proven character produces hope. This hope will not disappoint us, because God's love has been poured out in our hearts through the Holy Spirit who was given to us. (Romans 5:3–5 CSB)

WHAT THIS TRUTH MEANS FOR US

It's easy to want to give up in the middle of affliction. It's human to want to just call it quits when we are suffering. But the Bible gives us hope for enduring. When we suffer, we experience what Christ experienced. There is a unique and special union with Christ that takes place only in suffering.

Think about the new popular hobby of cold plunging. Specific neurotransmitters are released during these cold-water exposures, like serotonin, cortisol, dopamine, norepinephrine, and beta-endorphin.[5] These all play a key role in emotion and stress regulation. The absence of these things is associated with depression, anxiety, and even emotional disturbances.[6] In a way, our suffering is like the resistance of trying to step into that freezing cold water. But when we find ourselves in the cold water, it is producing something good, even though it does not feel good in the moment. In a similar way, Paul said suffering produces endurance, character, and hope (Romans 5:3–5). The best part of all this is that our hurting hearts will be full of the Holy Spirit, who pours out His love onto us.

I (Lysa) want to encourage you to get a sticky note and use it to mark this place in the book. This isn't just a chapter to read; this is biblical encouragement I want you to sit with and turn to over and over again as needed.

Now, as we end, I want to pray for you.

Lord, there is power in Your name. So I speak Your name over and over and over again for my sister reading this right now.

Jesus, Jesus, Jesus over the suffering she has experienced. Jesus, Jesus, Jesus over the heaviness in her heart as she thinks about all the loss she has endured. Jesus, Jesus, Jesus over her precious children. Jesus, Jesus, Jesus over every one of her unanswered questions and everything she wishes she understood. Jesus, Jesus, Jesus over confusion, fear, hopelessness, and feelings of helplessness. I speak the name of Jesus over all, around all, in and through all. Let her see glimpses of You, Lord, in ways too powerful to miss. Wrap her in Your tender mercies. And help those around her know how to do their part in helping her in this journey she is on.

In Your mighty name, amen.

COUNSELOR'S CORNER WITH JIM

In my experience in counseling, many people have talked to everyone else about the difficulties and issues they're struggling with, but they have not gone vertical and talked directly to God, expressing their honest questions and emotions.

I often invite people I work with to pull out an empty chair and imagine talking with God sitting in that empty chair. If you think it, say it. God can handle it and wants you to express your deepest pain, feelings, and *why* questions. Then quiet your heart, allow your tears to flow, and listen to the tender words of compassion and healing God may be speaking to you. Remember, *listen* and *silent* have the same letters.

CHAPTER 6

Life Changes, but You Get to Decide How You Change

So much about your life will change because of divorce. And each change will bring with it different emotions. Some changes will feel like a relief. I (Lysa) remember, at first, I was so desperate for the hurtful chaos to stop that a quiet house was comforting.

But after a while the quiet turned into loneliness and fear.

The quiet moments left a void that my runaway thoughts rushed in to fill. I guess I'd been in survival mode for so long that my thoughts had been focused on the more obvious losses the divorce would bring my way rather than the microlosses that would unfold in time. And then those microlosses started to surface. These were changes I hadn't anticipated. I hadn't braced myself for. I hadn't realized they would topple me over in waves of unexpected grief.

Things like a new season starting for the show we used to

watch together. A notification in my inbox for a deal an airline was running on tickets for a trip we'd talked about taking one day. The firewood he'd stacked near the house that was dwindling and never getting refilled. A Christmas nutcracker collection he would add to each year being pulled out of the stored decorations. The unmade bed that was usually his daily chore to take care of. The event invitations still addressed to Mr. and Mrs. TerKeurst. The text about it being time for his next oil change. Running into friends I hadn't seen in a long while who, based on their questions about what "we" were up to these days, didn't know we were no longer together.

I wasn't scrolling through Instagram, shopping for pain by checking up on him when these situations happened. No, they just hit me in the middle of everyday life.

The painful realizations will happen.

A friend of mine who is in the early stages of divorce called me last week in tears because her husband had always folded the towels in a very distinct, perfectionistic way. That morning she'd opened her bathroom cabinet and realized she was down to the last few towels he'd folded and placed there. She had no idea that something like this would hit her the way it did. She cried all the way to work and then called me from her office parking lot. She couldn't process it because she had no way to anticipate it. On a random weekday morning, she had to face another change, another grief. I explained to her that this was normal and that I had very much experienced this same thing. It didn't take away her pain. That would have to work its way through her and eventually turn into more of a scar than an open wound.

Marriage is the intertwining of lives together, as closely as the threads of fabric. And in divorce the threads must be separated from one another. It's an impossible task to do without ripping and breaking many, many of the threads. Seeing what you'd worked so hard to join together now being shredded isn't just sadness. It's full-blown grief that must be observed, cried over, mourned through, and laid to rest over and over and over. Each time something happens that resurrects the intense feelings of another realized loss, a mini funeral is called for. A marked moment of you making the choice to lay down into an imaginary grave another thought, expectation, or hope for a future that will no longer be with this person.

This can go on for years. All the love that should be there has turned into something painfully strange. No matter how good or terrible the interactions post-divorce are, the death of a marriage is a loss that must be worked through, prayed through, and talked through with a therapist or other trusted friend who can help you process the grief.

The cure for grief isn't time. Although time helps with the intensity and frequency of the pain, it's not what will finally close chapters of your life. The cure is acceptance. It's a futile exercise to hope that by resisting reality the grief will dissipate. It won't. It will only twist your life into a chokehold of hopelessness.

I hadn't wanted to let go of the future I believed and dreamed we'd have. I didn't want to let go of our family being all together under one roof. I didn't want to let go of our kids being able to pop over to our house and get advice from Mom and Dad sitting at "our" kitchen table. But what made me not want to let go wasn't based in reality. I not only had to learn to accept what would never be; I had to learn to accept what was not true about our life in the years leading up to the divorce.

A big part of what made the grief process so long for me was that I kept romanticizing things about our life together in ways that didn't match reality. I was looking back and repainting those memories better than they actually were. I was having such a hard time letting go of the way things should have been—the way I had wanted them to be rather than the way they had actually played out in those years before the divorce.

I imagined these everyday life connections happening without the fear of seeing him on his phone and wondering who he was texting. I imagined them happening without all the anxiety from his secrets. I imagined them happening without the shock of him announcing he had another last-minute trip. I imagined them happening without him making me feel like I was the crazy one. I imagined them happening without me making excuses for him and having that sinking feeling that our life could implode at any minute.

I had to grab each of those romanticized memories and force myself to interject a healthy dose of reality into those moments. The reason I say healthy dose is because we don't want to take our thoughts to the opposite extreme and simmer in anger and thoughts of retaliation. But keeping my thoughts true to what life was actually like when we lived under the same roof was important. It was sometimes a brutal process to force myself to factor in painful but necessary realities so I could get a grip on learning to accept the loss called divorce.

When my friend called me about the grief over using the last of the towels her husband had folded, I challenged her to interject her thoughts with reality. Instead of imagining him placing those towels in her cabinet as a loving gesture of a faithful man, I challenged her to remember he was actively in an affair when he put those towels there. He could have been on the phone with his girlfriend when he put the towels there. He could have been thinking about the next time he would connect with her. Or, worse, he could have been folding her towels over at her house while my friend was completely unaware of what he'd been doing.

Maybe none of that happened with the towels. But if your spouse has been treating you in dishonorable ways, those folded towels (metaphorically speaking) aren't a pure gesture of love toward you. So remember to factor in reality when moments of nostalgia threaten to pull you into an emotional come-apart. You are missing the way your life *should have been* rather than the way it actually was. This doesn't mean you park your thoughts in all the bad that happened and get bitter over this. But it does mean you remember correctly so you stay in touch with reality.

Here's the second part of the advice I gave to my friend: "This is now an opportunity for you to decide how you want your towels folded. He doesn't get to make that decision from now on. If you like how he did it, then you can fold your towels the same way he did. Or you can come up with a completely different method. You can fold them squarely, you can roll them, you can fold them in more of a rectangular fold-over, or you can fold them into the shape of animals like they do on cruise ships. Or don't fold them at all today and just put them into a pile to deal with tomorrow. The point is, it's your choice. It's your opportunity to decide how you want your towels folded, your bed made, the trips you want to take, the food you want to make. And if you don't want to feel the pressure to cook ever again, you can choose to get acquainted with a food-delivery app and call it a day. Oh, and if you want to paint your bedroom a lovely shade of blush or a dramatic olive green he would detest, you go, girl."

None of this is meant to glorify divorce. It's just a reminder that, in the midst of so many changes feeling so very hard and heartbreaking, it doesn't have to be all bad. You get to decide how you'd like to color your world, organize your closet, and what channel to watch.

You get to choose how you will change.

Even more important than those external things are the internal happenings of your mind and heart. Your trauma isn't just what happened. It's what you now tell yourself because of what happened.

> **You get to choose how you will change.**

Here's the part where I wish we were together in person so I could lean across the table, hold your hand, and look straight through your beautiful eyes down the pathway to your soul and remind you: He no longer has the right to play a major role in the narrative of your life.

He lost that right when he let go of your hand.
He lost that right when he refused to stop his bad behaviors.
He lost that right when he promised things would be different but those promises were empty.
He lost that right when he proved he couldn't be trusted with your heart.
He lost that right when he made selfish choices and abdicated his role as a protector in your life.

Please personalize those five sentences and read them out loud as a declaration, using his name in place of "he."

Now, remember, just because your ex-husband let go of your hand, couldn't be trusted with your heart, and left you, it doesn't mean that God will. The Bible makes it clear that God is the one who will not leave. He is the one who will stand beside you in your grief. He is the one who witnesses your loneliness and will make

Himself known to you in those tough moments. He has a special tenderness for the brokenhearted (Psalm 34:18). And, most of all, remember that God loves you. To be loved by God means He will always seek your highest good. It doesn't mean He will take away the pain. But it does mean He will grow you through it so you can gain the perseverance you need to face everything you will face.

You haven't been treated with tender love in a long time. Your spouse wasn't seeking your highest good. Your spouse forgot what a treasure you are. Your spouse lost sight of what a gift you were to him. Your spouse lost his way and tried to sell you the lie that you weren't worth the work it would take for him to get healthy enough to deserve all the love you tried to give him. But God is different.

Imagine God taking your face in His hands and whispering to you over and over, "I love you. I love you. I love you." You don't have to work for God's love or prove to God you are worth loving. His love never comes with a question mark, only lots of exclamation marks. Let that be what changes you from here on out.

I keep thinking about a tv series based on the book *All the Light We Cannot See*. There's a poignant scene where a sister puts her hands on her brother's face before he is taken off to war. She says, "Don't let them change you."[1] That's what I want us to remember here in this season. Don't let them turn you into a bitter woman who has forgotten her worth and forgotten that she can fold her towels any old way she pleases. Yes, there will be changes happening all around you, but if you change, let it only be for the better.

Now, pray this special prayer:

Father,

You are so very good. You can be trusted. Help me mark the hard moments of this day with declarations of my trust in You. There is more to what I'm facing today than what my physical eyes can see. When my pain feels too deep and when I don't think I can take one more second of suffering, help me recognize Your plan and protection. Help me trade my unbelief for the beautiful relief that I don't have to figure this out. I just have to fix my thoughts on Jesus and how He will lead me. I mark this moment as a moment of trust. I declare I don't have to understand. I just have to trust.

In Jesus' name, amen.

COUNSELOR'S CORNER WITH JIM

Some of the most frequent questions I get from women are these: How long will I feel this way? How long will it hurt this badly? How long will it take before I stop crying? How long will it take for me not to be so terrified of my future? How long will it take to heal?

I can't give you a time frame. But I can tell you that grief is like a canoe, continually moving you *through* all the geography of your emotions. Sure, there are moments you may feel stuck after the divorce, or like you're in a cul-de-sac going round and round in circles. But grief is not your enemy. The canoe of grief and healing will take you where it goes. Remember, the preposition *through* is front and center, not *out of* or *over* but *through.*

Healing is a journey and, although it can't be summed up in a few bullet points, I do want to tell you about a few mile markers you will likely discover along the way. An important caveat here is that we now have a number of different paradigms for understanding the grieving process. So, as you consider your own process, think about how you may relate to or recognize these five stages of grief,[2] which I like to call, instead, the stages of healing: (1) denial, (2) anger (turned outward toward God or others), (3) bargaining, (4) depression (anger turned inward toward yourself), and (5) acceptance.

1. Denial

Here you are at the ground zero of the destruction of your marriage. This is a shattered dream you never wanted. Who would? Don't try to pole-vault over this stage. You are human, and this stage of denial is not just expected, it is necessary. During this stage, I encourage people to journal, writing out all their thoughts about the shock and awe of the devastation they are experiencing. Like Lysa talked about in her book *It's Not Supposed to Be This Way*, please don't do a spiritual bypass in this first stage of divorce grief. Sit with your thoughts and dialogue out loud with them.

2. Anger (Anger Turned Outward)

Your anger is a God-given emotion. Don't be afraid of it. Maybe you believe it is unhealthy or a sin to be angry toward your spouse or ex-spouse, others, or even God about your unwanted divorce. Remember, God already knows the thoughts and emotions you are thinking and feeling. Here is another powerful place to use journaling as a tool, or to use an empty chair you imagine the other person sitting in. Then, out loud, speak your truth. Yell if you want to. Your repressed anger and stuffed emotions can literally kill you. One article even says, "Unforgiveness is classified in medical books as a disease."[3] So get those thoughts and feelings out.

3. Bargaining

We've all done this. Either pleading with a person to change or begging God to make someone change. Maybe you've cried out to God and made promises like "God, if you'll do this, I promise to do that." The cost and pain of divorce is so high that sometimes you will do anything to save your marriage or die trying. Bargaining reveals what our honest desires are. When you're in this stage, I challenge you to write out what you really want—this can be what you want from God or others, or what you want for yourself. For example, pay attention to thoughts or even words of "If you would just do ______, then . . ." Writing these things out makes them real. And through honesty, we are ultimately led to a posture of surrender, where we acknowledge what we most desperately want, hold it up to God, and release it to Him.

4. Depression (Anger Turned Inward)

Here, the grim reality of the finality of divorce begins to sink in. Think about a heavy concrete block pressing down on a pillow. At this stage, your anger turns inward at yourself, or you start to feel like you're drowning in your sorrow. I invite you to proactively practice empathy and self-compassion in this stage. While this depression stage is a normal part of the grieving process of divorce, some may actually experience a true clinical bout with depression. Please seek professional help if your depression is overwhelming you.

5. Acceptance

Depression is like taking a seat, but acceptance is the process of going from seated to standing. Having journeyed through the previous four stages of grieving your divorce, in this stage you begin to come back to life. Be gentle with yourself and don't be surprised if, even a year later, you find yourself back in the other stages. This is a fluid process. But know that every time you find yourself at the stage of acceptance, you have taken the necessary time and patient steps to accept the reality of what happened to you. Remember, mental health is a commitment to reality at all costs. Yes, facing the reality of divorce is painful, depressing, and not fair. But now your future is before you, and the abundant life God has prepared for you is on the horizon.

CHAPTER 7

It's Time to Take the High Ground You Were Meant to Occupy

At one point in my journey through divorce, the loneliness was so intense that I (Lysa) dreaded waking up to face another day, with all its opportunities and issues, by myself. I wasn't alone in life. I definitely had friends and my kids, who were willing to help. But I was alone in carrying the responsibilities of my life.

Figuring out everything emotionally took so much energy that trying to figure out regular stuff just exhausted me—everything from taxes to who to talk to about an insurance claim. When something happened to my car, I wondered, *Should I file that with insurance or will the eventual rate increase due to this claim cost more than just paying for it myself?* And other times, it was *What do I do when my internet goes out and buttons need to be pushed to reset it, but I don't know where they are located?* Or *How do I turn the water off when there's a leak and it will take the plumber a couple of hours to get to my house?* Or *What do I do to prevent bugs from destroying the grass?*

On and on these tasks kept coming. And the script I kept repeating to myself was *I can't do this.* Over and over, I reinforced the defeating statement.

But it wasn't just tasks that were pulling me down; it was also the weight of being a parent. My dynamic with my ex-husband didn't allow for amicable coparenting. I desperately wanted this to be possible. But due to reasons beyond my control, it wasn't. Though our kids were over the age of eighteen, they still needed a lot of parenting and guidance during some very crucial years of their lives. No one but their mom and dad would ever really get them and understand the dynamics at play when shepherding their hearts through this devastating divorce. But in my situation, I felt like I was carrying this completely alone.

Even my friends, who were amazing at helping me process things when we were together, wouldn't be able to understand the gravity of all the dynamics, because the consequences wouldn't affect them in the same way they affected me. I once told someone it was like walking through a field of landmines, where I was on the ground but all my friends were in a helicopter above me. They could call out advice and love and prayers, which was amazing support, but they weren't the ones whose life could be blown apart with one wrongly placed foot.

And while all the things I just described were contributing to the hardship of being solo, the loneliness was also intense, because I no longer had my person. I was lonely at dinner. I was lonely driving home from work. I was lonely on the weekends. I was lonely planning the holidays. And the worst grief of all, I was scared I would wind up being the old cat lady whose house was covered in spooky vines with hoarding as my only hobby. Also,

I pictured a wart on top of my nose that got crooked with age. Pretty, huh?

So I went to see Jim to get help with this overwhelming loneliness I was feeling. He talked me through it and then advised me to let this season of loneliness be an important part of my healing. He wanted me to learn to sit in the quiet and listen and tend to the thoughts and feelings that emerged.

What?!

I had just told him how the loneliness was brutal and I didn't know what to do. And his answer was for me to go home and be alone with my thoughts and listen? I wanted Jim to make me feel better. Jim wanted to equip me to be better able to face the future.

I really despised his advice.

Until I listened to his advice.

Over time I grew to understand it.

And now I've grown to value it.

But understanding and valuing his advice took quite a while. At the beginning, sitting in the quiet was awful. I didn't want to feel the emotions that emerged when I got quiet. Busyness and noise had become my way to cope with the intensity of what I was walking through. My pattern had been to navigate around my emotions by taking them captive and tidying them up. That's how I'd interpreted the scripture "Take captive every thought to make it obedient to Christ" (2 Corinthians 10:5). In other words, I would take a thought that was full of big feelings, scold myself for having those feelings, figure out how a Christian should act despite these feelings, and shove down what was still hurting me. I guess I was hoping these feelings I stuffed down would just eventually go away over time. And I got really good at lying to myself about my real feelings, too, so I wouldn't even have thoughts that needed to be captured. I reasoned that was how to live out that verse.

Except it wasn't working.

The feelings I stuffed down didn't go away on their own. Sometimes these feelings and resulting thoughts turned into a sinking sense of defeat, pity, or a seething bitterness. Or, other times, when I least expected it, I would have out-of-proportion reactions to everyday occurrences that certainly didn't warrant an emotional tirade. I felt so defeated. I wondered if that happy, fun, and stable woman I once was, was lost forever. Have you ever wondered that too?

I want us to take a deeper look at the wise instruction contained in the fullness of that scripture, 2 Corinthians 10:5: "We demolish arguments and every pretension that sets itself up against the knowledge of God, and we take captive every thought to make it obedient to Christ." In my earlier applications of this verse, I was missing crucial aspects of the process. I wasn't factoring in that I was actually in a spiritual battle that was playing out in everyday life. And no part of what I'd been doing included me listening to Christ. No part of it included me being obedient to Christ. Though having a calmer and tidier response to my big feelings seemed to be more Christlike, my motivation hadn't really been about Christ. It had been about avoidance and control.

I was treating my feelings as if they were the problem rather than letting my feelings inform me of what the real problem was. And the only way my feelings can serve their proper function is if I make space for them to emerge in the safety of the quiet. Look, our feelings are surrounded with intensity, and if we don't let them emerge in a nonthreatening space, they can eventually explode outwardly or implode internally, leaving us depressed and feeling quite powerless.

Many of my thoughts that were emerging from my intense

feelings were absolutely "arguments and pretensions" that came in direct opposition to the Scriptures. I was believing lies about how my future was never going to be good. I was cosigning my fears that God wasn't really going to come through for me. And I was so fixated on the hardships I was in the middle of that I started believing that evil was going unaddressed by God.

Big feelings. Desperate thoughts. Wrong conclusions.

God is not disappointed in you for having these feelings. But He does want to direct you through His Word on what to do with these feelings and the resulting thoughts. I recognize that sometimes the thoughts come first that drive us to have intense feelings. The order of what comes first, the thoughts or the feelings, isn't as important as the thoughts we fixate on.

For example, we can think about the person who hurt us, and the more we think about them, the more the feeling of resentment builds. The feeling is being perpetuated by the thought in our minds. Or we can feel lonely, and our loneliness reminds us of the absence of that person. And then we fixate on their absence, which continues to fuel our loneliness. As you can see, the common denominator is the thoughts we focus on, because they fuel the emotions and behaviors we live out.

I'll keep saying this over and over, because it's so important: The trauma we've experienced is not just what happened to us. It's the narrative we now tell ourselves because of what happened. So it is absolutely crucial to take quiet moments and do the good work of not letting our feelings and thoughts run rampant.

I (Joel) love this quote from Lysa: "Our feelings should be indicators, not dictators."[1] I know for me, personally, when I am in the midst of big feelings, it's tempting to be driven and directed by them. When this happens, it feels like I'm running purely on impulse. The problem is, in all the impulse, my thoughts begin to shift from being concerned about honoring God to how I can satisfy my own needs. These thoughts can really get us into trouble as they create more chaos than calm in our lives.

When you read 2 Corinthians 10:4–5 in context, you realize that when Paul was talking about taking our thoughts captive, he was talking about spiritual warfare. The battleground is our mind. Paul used intentional military imagery to communicate how we are to process our thoughts and feelings in a way that honors God and benefits us. He set the stage with the wisdom of God actively taking ground against the Enemy and gave us a threefold progression of how we are to do battle: first, tear down; second, capture; and, finally, conform.[2]

1. Tear Down

When we face our thoughts that have run rampant, we have to make the intentional decision to remove any power or authority they may have in our lives. We tear them down by seeing them for what they are: thoughts that are misaligned with the ways of God. So we dismantle the thoughts by presenting the truth of the Scriptures.

In the context of a military battle, often whoever has the high ground wins. Similarly, Paul described these untrue thoughts as things that are "raised up," by which he meant "high" or "lofty." As long as these thoughts have the high ground in our lives, they will have power over us. The first thing we have to do is tear them down from their place of height so they can't control or manipulate us anymore. To do this, we have to go on the offensive, confront the lie, and exchange it for the truth.

For example, when we are in the midst of suffering, it can feel like this is the end of the story or that it will always be this hard. We can tear down this thought by reminding ourselves that God is always working for the good of those who love him and do according to his will (Romans 8:28). With this truth, we can confront the lie and tear it down from its place of power in our lives.

Remember, there is power in speaking the truth of God, even if our hearts haven't signed on to it yet, and even if we don't see immediate evidence of it playing out in our life. The power is in speaking the words of God out loud, not in suggesting how we want God to solve our issue with this verse right now.

2. Capture

Just tearing down the statement that is opposing God's truth is not enough. Now we have to intentionally capture it, because, left unattended, it will just build itself back up. In the Roman world, after you tore down strongholds, you put prisoners in prison where they couldn't do any more harm.[3] In a similar way, visualize yourself taking that thought, walking it to a prison cell, putting that thought behind bars, closing and locking the door, and leaving it there while you turn around and walk toward the truth.

Look at the previous example of thinking *It's always going to be this hard*. You've already spoken the truth over it. Now close your eyes and mentally picture yourself leading this thought, like you would a prisoner, to its cell. As you picture yourself closing the gate, feel that sense of victory as you realize you're on the other side of that locked gate. Take in the safety of knowing you can turn around and now walk without the entanglement of that thought the Enemy is using to try to defeat you.

3. Conform

We find victory over negative thoughts when we are so consumed by the truth of God's Word that our very thoughts start to conform to be more and more like His. In a way, the more committed we are to the way of Jesus, the more we deprive negative thoughts of the oxygen they need to survive. The outcome will be thoughts that have been conformed to Christ.

How do we do this? Take a verse and memorize it. This builds muscle memory and cuts off the oxygen for the particular lie you are countering. And it makes space for your new thoughts to be more in keeping with God's truth. The more we do this (tear down, capture, conform), the more natural it will become and the quicker we will keep the lies from living rent-free in our heads, taking us down a thought spiral, and making us the ones who wind up prisoners to that lie. If you need a verse to start with, go back to the previous chapter and memorize one of those!

Full confession from me (Lysa). I don't always think of doing what Joel just described. Sometimes a thought rushes in with such force that I'm an emotional wreck almost immediately. Once I got so triggered in my pain that I misread something one of my kids did. I lost it. Like, yelling-at-the-top-of-my-lungs lost it. And then I made a dramatic exit from their house. When I got into my car to go home, I wanted to squeal my tires just a tad to really add a cherry on the top of my drama. But I am no expert tire squealer. And I didn't realize that the gravel on their long driveway lined with trees wasn't going to work like asphalt. So, when I attempted the tire squeal, instead of going forward, my car spun sideways and the whole front bumper of my car ripped off when it hit a tree. I got out of my car, picked up the bumper, put it in the back of my car, drove home, and hid the bumper inside our storage room. As if no one was going to notice it missing from my car. Lovely. Way to go, Lysa.

I'm not implying at all that you would ever do something that required you to hide your car bumper in a storage closet, but a thought running wild causing an emotional flooding? Yep, this may happen to you as well. Instead of having these out-of-control moments and then feeling like taking your thoughts captive doesn't work for you, I want you to remember this is a practice. Which means you probably won't do this naturally at first, but don't give up. The more you practice this, the better you'll get at it. And the better you get at it, the more you'll start to feel this terrific sense of empowerment.

The one who refuses to live in a perpetual state of being stirred up by everything that comes her way each day will reap the benefit of taking her thoughts captive. And the payoff is huge. You will put yourself in the position to occupy the high ground. And the one who occupies the high ground is the one who usually wins. So don't sacrifice your position of strength by letting the one who is acting foolish bring you down to their level.

Let's go back to where we started. It can be excruciatingly lonely in the quiet. But sometimes quiet is the beginning of an anthem song called resilience. Will it be uncomfortable? Yes. But isn't that a big part of what it takes to heal? Proving to yourself that you can be uncomfortable and still pressing through until there is a breakthrough.

God is in the quiet. Lonely is His invitation away from distraction so we receive what we need from Him. And healing is what He is offering.

> Sometimes quiet is the beginning of an anthem song called resilience.

I once had someone tell me the best revenge of all is to go on from here and live a remarkable life. Let's start taking all the runaway thoughts that have been derailing us and instead spend our energy in more productive ways. Let's walk into the future with eyes wide open to see and experience new possibilities and new joys. And if you're too tired today to believe me, at least walk over to your window and look out, look up, and remember there's a much bigger world out there than the confines of the pain you've been living in.

Don't let your feelings and thoughts oppose this.

We are going to make it. You will. And I will. And the thousands of others reading this book at the very same time as you—they are going to make it too.

This doesn't mean we don't make space for our pain or that we pretend we are unscathed. No, we must tend well to our healing. Maybe we will walk with a limp for a while. That's okay. There's no rush to get somewhere. It's just one minute, one hour, one day, one week at a time. Time will move you forward; you just have to steer in a good direction.

Eventually, the lights will come back on. Eventually, that dark abyss won't be nearly as deep and daunting as it once seemed. Eventually, you'll find yourself putting on a record of good soulful music, looking at a magnificent sunset, and whispering, "Thank you, God, for leading me to this moment right here."

Ask me how I know.

It's not perfect. Nothing in life ever is. But the grief is a lot less. The intense loneliness has dissipated. My perspective about it all is a lot more settled down and at peace. My face has more laugh lines now than tear streaks. And my eyes are sparkling wide open.

COUNSELOR'S CORNER WITH JIM

One of the reasons taking our thoughts captive is so important is that our words frame the reality we live in.

As you tend to your thoughts, beware of the "itty-bitty pity committee" inside your head that keeps trying to confuse you or condemn you. You cannot change a single thing in your past or about your past marriage. And you certainly had no power to change your spouse. But the rest of your life is before you.

Of course, you will have moments when you feel emotionally triggered or activated going forward post-divorce. That's normal and expected. Remind yourself of the biblical truth every day and remember the powerful encouragement and admonition of Ephesians 5:16: "Redeeming the time [going forward], because the days are evil" (NKJV). In this verse, Paul was reminding us of the honest reality of hardship and ruin in this world caused by sin. Paul didn't want us to live with a defeated mentality. Rather, we have even more reason to "redeem the time," as the darkness of the world should create an urgency within us to redeem and restore all that is good.

Keep your eyes and mind on the windshield of your life, and only occasionally glance into the rearview mirror. Why not spend time thinking through what you want your future to look like? This doesn't mean you presume to know what God should do. Rather, it's opening your thoughts to good things you'd like to work toward in the future. It's making room for resilient thoughts.

Think of it this way: Every new invention someone creates is actually created twice. Once in a vision for what could be and then in reality through developing the actual product. Clinically speaking, if you can look forward to something in your future, dopamine (the motivation neurotransmitter) will be released, as opposed to the cortisol that is released during times of constant stress. You've spent enough time in the past processing the pain, and now it's time to look forward and envision what you want your new life to look like. Maybe you even want to create a vision board to display these things. Are there hobbies you want to pick up? Places you want to travel?

You've come out of a nightmare, and now it's time to give yourself permission to dream.

CHAPTER 8

Forgiveness Feels So Incredibly Unfair

If I (Lysa) were you right now, I'd want to skip this chapter. And many of my friends who have walked through this divorce journey would probably say the same thing.

So let's not start with forgiveness. Let's start with giving each other the gift of bearing witness to what we've been through. I want us all to pause and acknowledge the harsh, chaotic, heart-rending, and, for some of us, almost life-ending realities we've faced. If we don't get this out first, forgiveness will feel like a betrayal to our story. We can't start the forgiveness process by trying to convince ourselves that we are now okay with all that happened.

Maybe some people can do this. I could not.

It can feel excruciating to try to forgive the person who hurt you so deeply that it altered the course of your life. The unchangeable can feel unforgivable. Even if they wanted to right the wrongs, the damage of that season and how it affected you can't be undone. The trauma etched so deeply that it rewires how your brain processes information isn't easily fixed. The broken trust, harsh rejection, and shocking actions of this person you thought would never hurt you in this way have now opened your eyes to the reality that they are, in fact, capable of treating you this way. You can't unknow this, and probably will not forget it anytime soon, if ever.

Yes, redemption can happen. The power of Jesus is great, and massive rips in a relationship can be worked on and repaired. Some relationships can emerge on the other side with a resilient strength after restitution, repentance, and healing. And even if the marriage didn't survive, I've seen some couples go on to have a beautiful friendship years down the road.

Even so, the need for forgiveness to be a part of the healing process can make it seem like the only way any of this is possible is if you fake it. Or at least force it and hope that your heart one day catches up.

When I was in the middle of my divorce, even if I tried to say the words "I forgive you" as I mentally pictured the people who hurt me, it brought me no peace. It actually brought me the exact opposite, because I knew my heart wasn't really signing on to what my mouth felt obligated to say. Plus, my divorce, like so many others, was a drawn-out process where new hurtful things kept happening. I could hardly catch my breath before I would learn another painful truth or realize another harsh reality that had me clutching my chest and trying to swallow the tears. Every day felt like divorce-awareness day, hitting me with waves of consequences, new realities I didn't want, and fears over the future that would sometimes render me emotionally paralyzed.

I remember the first Christmas where it was just the kids and me. We were sitting in the den, about to open gifts, when a text message popped up on one of the kids' phones. It was a picture of my ex-husband standing on the end of a pier jutting out to tropical water with not a cloud in the sky. He had his arms raised high and a huge smile on his face. None of us knew where he was. None of us knew who he was with. All we knew was that he was out traveling the world, seemingly living his best life.

I kept trying to pep rally my attitude, telling myself that I was the one who was blessed because I was the one with our kids. And that was very true. But it still hurt. The man I thought I knew would never have wanted to miss Christmas. He would never have wanted to cause his kids such confusion and pain. And yet this year he wasn't going to invite the kids over to his place. He wasn't going to watch them open gifts. He wasn't going to do any part of Christmas as they'd always known it. It was still a shock that this was where we were as a family.

I know some of my divorced friends had the opposite issue. Their ex wanted the kids for Christmas, which meant they would be alone on a day that had previously been all about family togetherness. That was extremely painful as well. Regardless of how this type of scenario plays out, all these changes seem incredibly unfair. The hurt just keeps coming to your present-day reality. Not to mention the triggers that come from past memories that suddenly feel like the crushing pain is happening right here, right now. The point is, it's so hard to forgive and move forward when the past won't stay in the past.

But Jim helped me so much with this, teaching me how to understand my resistance to forgiveness. The biggest realization was that I would most likely never have that epic conversation I was longing for, where my ex-husband finally owned all of what he did, apologized, and said that he wished he could take it all back.

I wanted that conversation.

I kept wanting that conversation.

Even when I no longer prayed we could repair things and put our family back together, I still kept thinking about how much I needed a conversation like that before my heart could really sign on to truly forgiving him.

How do you forgive someone who doesn't think they need, and who doesn't want, your forgiveness?

You reframe *why* you are forgiving that person. And Jim helped me see that.

By forgiving them . . .

- *You are not letting them get away with what they did.*

  People need to be held accountable for the choices they make. Sometimes it will feel like they are getting away with it, because we are suffering the consequences for their choices more than they are. That makes it tough to now say that, on top of everything else, you need to forgive them. But just remember, you aren't releasing them from God holding them accountable. You are releasing yourself from their actions holding you hostage with chains of bitterness. God will not be mocked by their sin. He will address it in His way and in His timing.
- *You aren't minimizing what they did.*

  Forgiving them doesn't mean that you now think what happened was no big deal. Their actions had a profound impact on you and many others. It's okay to still acknowledge that.
- *You aren't declaring that you've decided to forget all they did and drop the necessary boundaries you put in place.*

  Forgiveness is a command by God, but reconciliation is not. If they aren't repentant, it's okay for you to have boundaries in place that keep you safe, sane, and able to hold yourself together while you continue to heal.

- *You aren't saying that you want to reestablish a close relationship with them.*

  I once was told by someone who claimed to know what the Bible says that forgiveness wasn't real if I didn't reconcile with the one who hurt me. The Bible does not say that. In fact, the Bible doesn't say we have to stay in proximity to that person at all. Sometimes people assume they know what God's Word says. And sometimes those assumptions are wrong. When Jesus said we need to forgive seventy times seven (Matthew 18:21–22), it wasn't a directive to reconcile with a person who will keep hurting you. Again, it is okay for you to keep enough distance from this person so that, if they don't change, you can keep forgiving them from afar without getting destroyed in the process.

Now let's ask ourselves a really important question: Why are we forgiving that person?

Because forgiveness is God's prescription for the hurting human heart to heal. Forgiveness is not giving the person who hurt you a free pass. No, it's the process by which you receive God's gift of healing.

> Forgiveness is God's prescription for the hurting human heart to heal.

You deserve to stop suffering because of what another person has done to you. It's time to detach your ability to heal from choices your offender may never make. And it's time to be better prepared to step into your future with clarity and resilience.

Just this morning, I was reading Luke 23, one of the gospel

accounts of the crucifixion of Jesus. I was struck by something I hadn't realized before. In this passage, Jesus was modeling for us what to do when the actions of other people are creating life-altering circumstances:

> When they came to the place called the Skull, they crucified him there, along with the criminals—one on his right, the other on his left. Jesus said, "Father, forgive them, for they do not know what they are doing." And they divided up his clothes by casting lots. The people stood watching, and the rulers even sneered at him. They said, "He saved others; let him save himself if he is God's Messiah, the Chosen One." The soldiers also came up and mocked him. They offered him wine vinegar and said, "If you are the king of the Jews, save yourself." There was a written notice above him, which read: this is the king of the Jews. (vv. 33–38)

"Father, forgive them" were his first words uttered from the cross, not his last words. Let's think about that for a minute. The first recorded statement Jesus speaks from the cross is centered on forgiving those who were causing such pain in that very moment.

Nothing was solved.

Nothing was getting better.

As a matter of fact, shortly after Jesus asked God to forgive those crucifying Him and rallying against Him, we read that soldiers offered Him wine vinegar. This was such an offensive and disgusting gesture. Roman soldiers were required to carry with them sponges soaked in wine vinegar to clean themselves after defecating.[1] This is what they offered up to Him to drink in the midst of His extreme suffering. And others were mocking Him, devaluing Him, belittling Him, and treating Him worse than a criminal worthy of execution, though He'd never sinned.

I don't know all the reasons Jesus made this statement of forgiveness right in the midst of being brutalized. But I can tell you what forgiveness, even while hurting, has done for me:

- *Forgiveness made me feel a sense of autonomy in my weakness.*

  So much of what was happening was out of my control. But my choice to forgive was my opportunity to take a stand for my healing. (For more on God's forgiveness and how it brings healing, see Psalm 103:3–4. Also see Genesis 45:1–28 to read how Joseph's forgiveness of his brothers set him free to do the will of God and be a blessing.)
- *Forgiveness helped me find some good where there seemed to be very little going my way.*

  Unforgiveness will not lead us toward a better future. It will leave us circling the wrongs done to us over and over in our thoughts and in our conversations. Forgiveness helped me focus less on what happened and more on the transferable wisdom I was gaining from going through the situation at hand. (For another example of God working out eventual good in situations that don't seem good, see the story of Abigail and David in 1 Samuel 25. Abigail pleaded for David to forgive her husband's offense [v. 28]. David chose forgiveness, which ultimately led to a better future not only for himself but also for Abigail.)
- *Forgiveness was a marked moment when I knew I was being obedient to God.*

  I've often challenged myself when I feel stuck to go back to the last time God instructed me to obey Him and make sure I've done what He wanted me to do. To forgive is to please God, and it positions us in His will, living out His Word (Colossians 3:13).

- *Forgiveness allowed me to be used by God to truly take what was meant for evil and use it for good.*

  None of what I went through felt good. But helping others through this tragedy has brought good into my life. The pain was not pointless. In fact, the pain actually pointed me toward an even greater sense of purpose. (For more on this, see Genesis 50:20 and read about Joseph's story.)

Another aspect of Jesus' forgiveness statement from the cross is that He wasn't just asking the Father to forgive the people involved for what they *had done*. He was also asking the Father to forgive them for what they were *doing* and for what they were *about to do.* He was also offering forgiveness for you and me for the future sins we would commit, even though we weren't even alive yet. And in doing this, He was modeling for us what to do when we are also facing excruciating circumstances.

Forgiveness is not a burden He places on us when we are hurt by others. Forgiveness is the only way to keep us unburdened from the bitterness, rage, and desire for revenge that can so easily sneak into our hearts. Jesus doesn't want another person's wrongdoing to be multiplied within you or to be unleashed onto others by you.

Please don't hear me say that we will have the ability to immediately forgive like Jesus did on the cross. I want to give you permission to let the grace of God give you the time you need to process and wrestle and cry and feel all the natural feelings that may come up when you are being treated in demeaning and deplorable ways. But what I am saying is, don't wait for things to be made right before you take this step. Waiting for something that may never happen, like I said, is going to stunt your healing and growth.

I want to close this chapter by telling you a story about a friend of mine. My friend was going through a divorce, but because of legal reasons, neither she nor her soon-to-be ex-husband could leave the home. I don't understand this, but I've heard about this happening in many other cases. So, my friend slept in her daughter's room, and he slept in the master bedroom. During one particularly hard part of the divorce process, my friend's mother came to offer some help with the kids. Over the course of that week she was visiting, the mother became increasingly disturbed and angry with how unfair it was that the soon-to-be ex-husband had taken the master bed and her daughter was sharing a much smaller bed with one of the kids. One day, after he'd left for work, the mother couldn't take it any longer. Without anyone knowing, she slipped into his room, pulled back the sheets, and dumped an entire bag of sugar in his bed. She remade the bed and said not a word. The next morning, he came into the kitchen infuriated and demanding to know who had put "sand" in his bed. The mother stood up proudly and proclaimed, "It wasn't sand; it was sugar. And you deserve that and so much more!"

Every time I think about that story, I laugh. No real harm was done, but it sure did make his bed terribly uncomfortable. What was that mom really doing? She was trying to level the scales. That mom wanted him to suffer a restless night of sleep, just like her daughter had done for so many nights because of his actions.

Please hear me before you run to your pantry and grab a bag

of sugar. It didn't make anything better. It only made him feel validated and gave him an example to use when he was telling others about how "crazy" my friend and her mother were.

Her husband had been a cruel man. He would often punish my friend by not speaking to her and refusing to acknowledge her presence. Once he did this for six months straight. And my friend didn't even know what she'd done. It was excruciating and left her mind reeling with questions about what he might be hiding or covering up during his long stretches of silence. It wasn't fair. None of what she endured for years and years was fair. And certainly the way the divorce played out and left her financially devastated was not fair.

The truth is, when you're staring across the great abyss of the unknown called divorce, not much is going to be "fair." If fair is the goal we decide we must reach before we pursue forgiveness, we might be chasing something that can't ever be caught. The exhaustion of living that chase day after day is a quick way to find yourself bitter and stuck. In trying to seek fairness, you might inadvertently experience the most unfair outcome of all: turning into someone you were never meant to be.

I know this is hard. If you're still angry and frustrated and wanting to scream from the mountaintops about how wrong all this is, I get it. I know it's tough to navigate the present realities of all that's been taken. I know it's like a stab to the heart to see your ex moving on with another woman so quickly while you're still picking up the pieces of your broken heart. I know custody issues are brutal and financial strains are real. I know seeing the one who hurt you so deeply skipping into the future with seemingly no consequences is maddening. Yes, yes, a million times yes, it is unfair. But your strategy at this point can't be to make things fair. It's time to start making things right for your future.

This story is unfinished. And if you are withholding forgiveness because it feels like the only way to punish the one who hurt you, chances are they aren't learning any lessons or becoming a better person because of your unforgiveness. When this revelation hit me, I wondered, *So will he just get away with all he did?* The answer is no. God will not be mocked (Galatians 6:7). Sin will not go unaddressed forever.

The Enemy wants to destroy us. God wants to redeem us. And it's in that moment, when forgiveness is our choice, that we win. We turn from darkness. We refuse the Enemy's invitation. We follow Christ's example. And we walk toward the light of Jesus' redemption, where healing will be found.

COUNSELOR'S CORNER WITH JIM

As Lysa said, sometimes what makes forgiveness feel so hard is that the one who hurt you refuses to own what they did, admit they were wrong, and offer any kind of restitution. While you can forgive this person without them acknowledging their need for forgiveness, I want you to take great caution if you are still in a close relationship with this person. I'm going to say something challenging right here, but please know it's for your good: You cannot be in a healthy flourishing relationship with someone who refuses to take responsibility for their own issues. This is a big statement, but it's a true statement.

That's why I want to include information about something called "the victim triangle" here at the end of this chapter on forgiveness. It can help you see why forgiveness doesn't have to be about them at all. It can help *you* get free of the suffering they have caused you and be better equipped not to keep living in this exhausting dysfunction. The goal here is to help you find freedom. It might not be freedom from this person. If you have close contact with them, that may be tough. But I do want to help you break free from participating in their toxicity. One way to do this is to recognize if you are getting assigned a role in their life that you don't want to sign up for.

The victim triangle was developed by psychiatrist Stephen Karpman in 1968. Karpman observed the interactions and transactions between people in relationships and noted three overall roles: the victim, the rescuer, and the persecutor (I use the term *perpetrator*). Each of these roles has a specific function and payoff. Let's take a closer look at them.

The Victim

The victim in the triangle was typically victimized in some way in their past. They often don't do the deeper work in therapy to address the facts and impact of how they were hurt, abused, abandoned, or betrayed. Remember: What people don't work out they will act out. The victim will look at others in their lives through a magnifying glass and will avoid looking or refuse to look in the mirror at themselves and their own issues. They want two specific people in their life, the one who will rescue them and the perpetrator they can blame.

The Rescuer

The rescuer typically is a people pleaser. Many times, these rescuers played the role of peacekeeper in their family of origin. Rescuers are secretly driven by anxiety and fear. Yet, in contrast to this inner insecurity, they put on the cape and tights and go to great lengths to "save" people from their bad choices and unhealthy ways of living. This is why, in my counseling work, I always do a deep dive into a person's life story, especially those crucial developmental years. Often, I have discovered a counselee had a sibling or parent who was emotionally unhealthy, addicted, rebellious, or simply irresponsible. In reaction to these realities, these developing rescuers could not manage their own internal anxiety and discomfort, so they consciously or subconsciously rose up to cover, explain, or distract from the failure and excuses of others.

While many may perceive these rescuers as humble, gracious, caring servants, there is more going on than meets the eye. Yes, they may be kind, compassionate, and service-minded, but a deeper look at their motives and mode of operating can reveal a pattern of unhealthy control of others. The idea here is "I know what is best for you." This unhealthy "other-centeredness" often comes at the cost of a lack of self-care, self-awareness, and self-compassion.

The Perpetrator

The final player is the perpetrator. Sometimes these are legitimate villains who have been and continue to be cruel to the victim. While this is awful, the victim has a choice to exercise agency (more on that later).

Yet, other times, the one assigned the role of the perpetrator isn't the real villain at all. They've simply been acting with boundaries and self-care. They become a villain when they don't give the victim what they want, how they want it, and when they want it. They aren't being selfish; they are being realistic with their own limited areas of capacity. Remember, in order for a victim to continue to be the victim, they have to have a bad guy in their story. Victims need these "bad guys" to be bad, so they have someone to blame everything on and so they don't have to take ownership of their own issues.

How do you get out of this toxic dance of the victim triangle? No matter which role you may play, your own self-awareness is the first step to exit the triangle. Do your own honest self-assessment of your involvement in the triangle. Pray and ask God to help you see what you need to see. Talk with a counselor or a trusted friend about what historical unhealed hurt or trauma might be fueling your specific role in the triangle. And, last, be prepared for the fact that, if you have been in this rescuer role and you now start drawing necessary healthy boundaries, the one with the victim mentality may shift you into the role of a perpetrator. This isn't because your boundaries are bad. It's because an unhealthy person has never met a boundary that they like.

If you are in the victim role, take ownership of what is your responsibility. Admit your own faults and refuse to blame anyone else. This is known as agency. If you are in the rescuer role, start practicing healthy boundaries with consequences, be willing to say "no more" and allow the victim to experience the consequences of their choices and lack of responsibility.[2] If you are in the perpetrator role, be honest about whether you have wronged the victim in any way. If you have, seek forgiveness. If they are finding fault in you because you drew some healthy boundaries, don't own what isn't yours to own. Recognize what's really going on here. The one with the victim mentality is accusing you of being their perpetrator so they may build the case that they were the victim, are the victim, and can continue to be the victim. When they blame you, they are discharging their pain by making it always someone else's fault.

Whichever role you find yourself in, consider, when possible, seeking outside mediation with a therapist, a pastor trained in recognizing this dynamic, or safe friends. No matter what, it is each person's responsibility to take ownership of their actions and to get out of the triangle, whether the other people stay in the triangle or not. And how do you do this? You step out of the unhealthy role you've been playing and refuse to continue to adjust your life because of an unhealthy person's commentary and demands.

CHAPTER 9

But I Feel Like a Forgiveness Failure

Jim asked me (Lysa) a profound question in one of our sessions: "Do you want to heal?" I lowered my head and whispered, "Yes." And then he said we should work on forgiveness.

No part of me felt ready to sign on to that yet. I just wanted him to say some things in our session to make me feel better. I was so tired. I didn't want to have to do anything that day. Forgiveness felt like such a heavy lift. No thank you.

Jim didn't push me. He just handed me a stack of three-by-five cards and said, "Let's just start by listing out what has caused you so much pain. Write each painful thing done or said to you in this situation on individual cards and place them around the floor."

That wasn't hard. I started on the first card and was surprised by how quickly the floor was covered with these cards. Seeing all that pain written out and staring back at me helped me understand why I felt so heavy inside. It was a lot. Too much to continue to carry.

Jim was quiet for a bit while he read the words I'd written. I could feel myself getting choked up as I watched him go from card to card, because I could tell Jim really felt for me. He wasn't reading the cards as a clinician. He was reading them as a fellow human. He then looked at me and told me that he believed me. And that what happened was wrong. Very wrong. He acknowledged my suffering and believed these facts that I was sharing without questioning me about any of it. He then said something that profoundly helped me: "Lysa, if the one causing this pain never says they are sorry for what they did, I will. I'm so sorry you've endured all of this pain."

When he did this, something good broke loose inside me. The resistance no longer had such a strong grip on me. I could feel my heart soften and the tension in my muscles release. It wasn't that everything felt right at that moment. But what a powerful thing it was to have another human bear witness to my pain. I realized I didn't need the person who hurt me to do it. I just needed someone to stand beside me and validate how wrong these betrayals were.

I guess my ultimate resistance with forgiveness was my fear that if I released being so angry about what happened, there would never ever be any righting of these wrongs. But when Jim agreed with me that all I'd suffered was so terribly wrong, it was a moment of justice for me. He knew the facts of my situation better than anyone and, though he wasn't picking sides, he was standing with me in this moment of truth.

I wasn't crazy.

These things done and said to me were awful.

I deserved better than this.

And a person trained to see and recognize the truth acknowledged the severity of what I had endured.

That's when I decided I no longer wanted to be the one who had gotten hurt. I wanted to now be the one who had gotten healed.

Jim then explained to me that every trauma has two parts: "fact and impact" (remember the Trauma Egg exercise); therefore, there are two parts to forgiveness as well. When we experience trauma, we always need to deal with the fact of what happened. But then there's also the impact of the wrongs done to us. This is how this trauma will now affect us and the price we will now pay because of someone else's actions.

When we are instructed by God to forgive, we can be obedient to that command by having a marked moment in time where we verbalize our choice to forgive the person for the *facts* of what they did. But there is a second part that so many of us miss. We also have the freedom to take a much longer healing journey toward forgiving for the *impact* this has had on us. While forgiving for the fact can happen as quickly as we choose it, forgiving for the impact should take and will take as long as we need.

While forgiving for the fact can happen as quickly as we choose it, forgiving for the impact should take and will take as long as we need.

Have you ever said you've forgiven someone but then, a few days later, something triggers the pain you still feel and bitterness against that person stirs up all over again? And then on top of everything else, you feel like a forgiveness failure? You can start to believe that somehow forgiveness just doesn't work for you. But that's not what's happening.

When you get triggered, that's an indication of more of the

impact being revealed to you. This revelation doesn't mean that your choice to forgive that person didn't stick. Or that it didn't count somehow. No, it just means you are now faced with the choice to deal with this impact, to have another marked moment of forgiveness around what this trauma is continuing to cost you.

After Jim explained this to me, I felt ready to walk through forgiving my offender for the facts of what they'd done. It gave me such relief to know I could be obedient to God with this marked moment in time. But I could also still have space to process the feelings that would come when more and more of the impact would hit me.

This is the script I used: "I am making the choice to be obedient to God and forgive this person for this fact of how they've hurt me. And whatever my feelings will not yet allow for, the blood of Jesus will surely cover it." With that, Jim gave me pieces of red felt to cover each card as I got to it.

I now have a marked moment in time to look back on and can rest assured I have forgiven the person who hurt me. And when the triggers come, I've learned what to do with them after processing the pain and acknowledging I may need more healing around this revelation. I then use the same script from above, only changing it slightly. I close my eyes and whisper, "Out of obedience to God, I've already forgiven this person for the fact of what they did. But now I am also choosing to forgive them for this part of the impact I'm now experiencing. And whatever my feelings will not yet allow for, the blood of Jesus will surely cover it."

This exercise was one of the most important parts of my healing. It helped not just with processing the hurts with my ex-husband but even more with processing all the other relational hurt I experienced during this season.

One of the issues with divorce tragedy is that some people

around you won't know what to do with this implosion of your life. Most people know what to do when someone you love passes away. There's a protocol of sorts. They come visit you. They bring you food. They come to the memorial service. They watch the video to celebrate the life that was. They feel deeply for your loss. It hits something personal deep inside them, and they cry alongside you. Then they go to the burial service. They accept the ending. They give you space to heal. They give you grace and time off, and they understand if you can't show up for a while. And they don't judge you for the loss or wonder what you should have done better. Nor do they attempt to resurrect what is gone and make you feel guilty for not doing the same.

Yes, many people know what to do when there's been a death. However, most people don't know what to do when there's been a divorce. People have opinions and reactions that may surprise and hurt you.

I was so caught off guard by this. I thought I had a pretty good feel for how certain people would react. For a good number of them, I predicted correctly. But others reacted in ways that shocked me. Some of their reactions added a lot of grief on top of my already broken heart.

I don't want to draw your attention to this to make you afraid or even more skeptical of others around you. Maybe the majority of the people in your life will attempt to lessen your sorrow and not add to it. But if that's not the case, I want to help you be better prepared than I was. And if you've already experienced this, maybe it will help you to know how to better frame the hurt they caused and work toward forgiveness for them as well.

Looking back now, I can see that people who added pain in the midst of my divorce process fell into five different reaction categories:

- *Those who added to the confusion by making up the reasons this happened with my marriage.*

  This group didn't necessarily blame me, but I think they felt if they could identify the reason this happened, they could somehow prevent it from happening to them. In other words, they hoped that as long as they didn't make the same mistakes, they would be safe from divorce happening to them. And, look, I don't fault them for the fear that led to this kind of rationale. But it sure did teach me not to jump to conclusions just to ease my own mind when other people go through hardships.
- *Those who added to my pain by blaming me.*

  One person was convinced I caused my ex-husband to have an affair because I traveled for work. Another person said it was because I'd gained weight (ugh . . . that one really hurt). And another said my success made him feel overlooked. All these issues would have been things to discuss if they were bothering him. Or possible reasons to go to marriage counseling. But in no way did they justify the choices he made to step outside of our marriage. Regardless, some people seemed to want to blame me for "driving him to this bad place." They determined there had to be some sort of cause and effect at play for a "good man to make such unexpected choices." My thought about this now is that I'm not that powerful. I'm not powerful enough to drive someone from healthy to unhealthy. Yes, I can own my issues. But I will not own the wrongdoings of another person.
- *Those who disconnected because they didn't want to be involved.*

  Whatever the reason people stayed silent, their hands-off approach made me feel like I was alone in an intense battle against darkness that was devastating me and had such a grip on my then-husband. While a few of our friends did attempt to encourage him to live up to the Christlike standard he professed, sadly, many others stayed silent.

- *Those who minimized the impact this was having on me and the kids and were bound and determined to convince me to stay no matter what.*

  I'll keep emphasizing this over and over: Marriage is something to be taken very seriously. The vows we take at the altar are meant to be kept. Yes. But encouraging someone to stay when they are in a marriage where one party is exhibiting destructive patterns of behavior and refusing to change, causing extreme distress to their spouse and possibly the kids, too, or abandoning their family and refusing to care for them—this is not what honors God. We honor what is honorable. Like Joel has said before, we should not elevate the institution of marriage over the well-being of the spouse being hurt over and over.

- *Those who didn't want to see him face the consequences of his choices and treated him as the victim.*

  I found this to be the most distressing of all the reactions. Usually this would happen when I had to draw necessary boundaries that others didn't understand or agree with. These boundaries weren't motivated by a desire to retaliate. These boundaries helped me communicate what was no longer acceptable with our relationship and helped keep me safe and sane. The one making the destructive choices is not a victim of his or her decisions. They may be the victim of abuse or abandonment or some very hurtful actions that happened earlier in life, but, as an adult, it is their responsibility to get help for their issues.

None of this is meant to sound like I'm judging anyone. It's just an observation that even some well-meaning people won't get it. That doesn't mean they don't love you or that they can't get there one day. It's just that they don't fully get what you're facing right now. Remember, as Jim often says, "People are down on what they're not up on."

I do need to take a minute to applaud friends who offered true care and sincere compassion. Thankfully, there were enough of these friends to help balance out the others. Most of these people had been through some kind of brokenness themselves, and they knew that life just falls apart sometimes.

They offered practical help. They sincerely prayed more words over my divorce than they spoke about my divorce. They were trustworthy and didn't gossip. They believed I was telling the truth. They sought to understand where I was and what I was facing on a daily basis. And if they needed to challenge me, they did it without an ounce of judgment. They gave me advice but then also gave me space to make my own decisions. I am forever grateful for those kind souls who loved me and my kids so well.

With those who either intentionally or inadvertently compounded the pain I was in, it would've been easy to walk away and not deal with them. But I started to realize that my healing journey would never be able to keep moving forward if I still carried threads of bitterness and frustration toward those people in my heart.

There is never just a little bit of bitterness.

There is never just a little bit of anger or frustration or resentment.

Those things don't just want to be one feeling in our hearts; they want to become the consuming feeling.

Maybe for you it's been easier to distance yourself from some of the people who hurt you, and you thought distance would fix the problem. Please understand that forgiveness is not necessarily about reengaging with all these people. This may not be possible or safe to do. But consider the good that might come about in your own heart if you pulled out some three-by-five cards and let the forgiveness journey continue.

COUNSELOR'S CORNER WITH JIM

Get a piece of paper and write down some of the statements people have made to you about where you may have been wrong in your relationship, including those from your ex-spouse or spouse. Maybe you've even been in agreement with these statements or accusations. As you write them down, don't edit yourself. Then, once you're done, go back and run them through the filter of truth and reality. I'm going to ask Lysa to provide a little more insight here.

Here's a practical example from when I (Lysa) did this. I told you there was a person who believed that my ex-husband cheated because I traveled for work.

Okay, did I travel? Yes.

Did I travel too much? My ex-husband helped set my schedule and was very involved with determining what engagements I said yes and no to.

Did his concerns about me traveling ever come up in the many joint counseling sessions? No.

Now, could I have reevaluated my travel once I knew our marriage was in trouble to give us the necessary time to get help? Yes. And I did.

Again, were there things I needed to own that contributed to the dysfunction? Yes, of course. I'm so very human, and I have my own areas of weakness and brokenness. But I had such a propensity to own things that were not mine to own that it was necessary for me to work on this not being my natural inclination going forward.

I (Jim) just want to say, especially for those of you who, like Lysa, tend to own more than what is yours to own, this method of running what people say to you through the filter of truth and reality is a healthy ongoing practice to incorporate into your life. When something new comes up, when someone says something to you that feels painful, take a step back to work through the whole situation and own what is yours to own but no more. When you do need to own something, know that this isn't a statement about who you are as a person but rather an acknowledgment of a mistake you've made that you want to stop before it becomes a pattern. This is a freeing exercise to add to your repertoire and one that can help you in all your relationships.

CHAPTER 10

What Does Accepting This New Normal Look Like?

Today I (Lysa) opened my Instagram and immediately saw a post from someone I don't follow, and it startled me. I don't know why it seems Instagram is sending me more content from people I don't follow than people I do follow. It caught me off guard to see this, because it brought to the forefront of my mind a person who is the representation of a lot of past pain in my life.

I closed my phone and sat with what I'd just seen. Instead of letting my mind spin off into unhealthy thoughts, I immediately used my anxious energy differently. I took inventory of my thoughts and feelings.

Someone in my life always reminds me, "You might not have control over your first thought, but you should absolutely take control over your second thought." So I asked myself some really important questions:

- *What am I feeling?*
- *What is feeding those feelings?*
- *Without tidying anything up, what was my first thought when I saw this?*
- *What would it look like to process this feeling through the lens of hurt and bitterness?*
- *Would there be any good, long-term outcome of that reaction?*
- *What would it look like to process this feeling through the lens of maturity and healing?*
- *What would be the benefit of doing that?*

Six years ago, this situation would have sent me into full-blown anxiety and whatever I had scheduled for that day would have to be rescheduled. I would need someone I trusted to process this with me and assure me the emotions I was having were understandable.

But today was different.

Here's how I answered those questions:

- *What am I feeling? I was feeling odd.*
- *What is feeding those feelings? I was caught off guard to see this person in my Instagram feed.*
- *What was my first thought? She doesn't belong here.*
- *What would it look like to process this feeling through the lens of hurt and bitterness? I would want to mentally criticize her and cast her as a villain.*
- *Would there be any good, long-term outcome of that reaction? It might feel good to be brutally honest in the short term, but in the long run that would only bring more negativity into my mind and put me in a bad mood.*

- *What would it look like to process this feeling with maturity and healing? It would make me feel good, because I wasn't handing her the power to ruin my mood, my day, or my outlook.*
- *What would be the benefit of doing that? I could see the situation for the brief interruption that it was and then close my phone to do something more productive.*

After some time had passed, I called a very close friend to tell her what had happened. And the feeling I had after having time to sit with it all surprised me. I had compassion for the woman in the Instagram post.

I found this to be a little unexpected. Maybe a bit odd. She had taken something from me. Yes. But she was also now living in the chaos God delivered me from. And it was with that revelation that compassion bubbled up to the surface. It was real. And I wasn't pretending or tidying up my real feelings. This compassion was honest. And just for this slice of time, I loved that this is where my feelings and thoughts landed. Who knows if I'll always feel this way? I'm not going to put the pressure on myself to always feel something "right and good" from now on. Nope. Healing is a fluid thing that ebbs and flows and will last the rest of my life. But I was happy to receive this moment as a really good sign for right now. This was a lot less about her and more about gauging where I'm at and how my heart is doing on this random Tuesday in the middle of a very cold January.

Last week, I was out to lunch with some friends, and one of them asked me what the number one thing was that I did to help with my healing. I rambled for a bit but then landed on one powerful word: *acceptance*.

I replied back to her, "I've finally accepted my life." This wasn't a resignation. Not at all. It was a declaration that I've made the decision to love my imperfect, messy, unpredictable, sometimes unfair, and sometimes unbelievably good life. I'm making peace with the fact that there will be very odd things about my reality that aren't at all the cookie-cutter norm. I'm making peace with what is now really hard because of this divorce. I'm making peace with the fact that I may never get answers to some really important questions. I'm making peace with what is, what isn't, and what I don't know about my future.

And the only way I'm able to work on making peace is by redefining what peace means to me personally in this season of life.

One day I was talking to my daughter and I was lamenting that I just wanted normal again. Without missing a beat, she said, "Mom, if you want that, then you need to redefine *normal* and redefine what peace will look like for you right now."

Normal can't be a return to the way things were. The way things were was dysfunctional.

Normal can't be a return to an idyllic vision of what I'd hoped my life would look like.

Normal can't be where all the wrongs are made right and the one who hurt me undoes all the damage he caused. I can't change what happened in the past.

Normal can't be what other people have or how other people live. Comparison doesn't help. They have their stuff to deal with too. No matter how rosy it all looks, it's still imperfect because their story is unfolding in an imperfect world too. A script I will often say is "I'm not equipped to handle her stuff, both good and bad, and it's always a packaged deal."

And normal can't be the dreams I used to have for my future. If I keep reaching for an unrealistic normal, peace will elude me.

Let me state that again. If I keep reaching for an unrealistic normal, peace will elude me. But if I choose to accept my life just as it is today, something shifts inside me. This acceptance is not me settling for less. It's actually me setting myself up for what's next.

It's me laying down my pride, thinking that I know what's best. It's me releasing what is out of my control. It's me realizing that life isn't always fair, but it can still be good—very, very good.

> Acceptance is not me settling for less. It's actually me setting myself up for what's next.

Remember at the beginning of this book how we were both asking how long will it take to heal? I finally have the answer.

It takes as long as it takes.

Healing isn't a finish line to reach but rather a process through which we discover our greatest strength.

You've been incredibly brave. And now I hope you feel even more prepared to continue the process of letting go while holding yourself together. I hope you can see that every tear you've cried was your pain leaving to make room for amazing possibilities. Your life isn't over. It's just at a new beginning, and I can't wait to see where you go from here.

COUNSELOR'S CORNER WITH JIM

Proverbs 11:14 reminds us, "Where there is no counsel, the people fall; but in the multitude of counselors there is safety" (NKJV). To establish this kind of safety, I encourage people to form what I call a personal board of directors.

In a way, Lysa, Joel, and I have played the role of your personal board of directors here in the pages of this book, but now we want to pass the baton for you to create that in your own life (and you may already have a version of this). Here's how to start.

Step One: Identify

Think about who these people might be. Sometimes it's just a few close friends. So you can have an example, I've asked Lysa to step in here.

Here is my personal board of directors as I (Lysa) was walking through my divorce:

- Two friends going through the same thing I was
- Jim, my counselor
- Joel, a trusted friend to study the Bible with who will shoot me straight with the truth
- A friend who loves the Lord and has therapeutic wisdom
- A friend who is good with finances and who can help me think through things like bills, estate planning, insurance, and other professionals we might need to contact
- My attorney
- Several friends who committed to praying for me

This list of people was personal to me based on the needs I had. Your list needs to include people unique to your needs and what is realistic for you. The point isn't to get it all perfect. The point is to get the help you need and to not go at this alone.

I never had a group meeting with all these people. But their collective wisdom helped me immensely.

When thinking through who to include, I identified what my most urgent and practical needs were and the kind of support I needed in that season of my life and filled those roles as best I could. I'm still very much in touch with each of these people, even though it's been years since my divorce. Now our check-ins are less intense and urgent than they once were. But each of these people was crucial in helping me then and they continue to help me make prayerful, informed decisions. I relied on this board for a lot of encouragement, prayer, and support. It felt good to have people who I knew were for me, especially when others misunderstood me and my situation.

Step Two: Ask

Once you've identified the right people, I (Jim) want you to ask these people to come around you. Ask them questions like these: What do you see? What am I missing? What am I not seeing? Do you see any area where I am resistant to wisdom, reality, or something else? What do you see me doing right? What are some scriptures you've read recently that may help me right now? And as you do this, remember a few things:

- These friends are here to support you and help you, but don't be afraid to have them sometimes challenge you.
- They are here to help you carry the weight. So let them in rather than try to carry it all yourself.
- They will help you stay committed to the best version of yourself, in a season where your emotions could get hijacked often.
- They can't support you without knowing where you're hurting. Consider inviting them to hear your Trauma Egg or life story, or at least maybe the top five to ten areas of woundedness from your past.
- They will likely have things going on in their own lives, too, so leave room for people to come on the board and off the board (for different reasons, like seasons of life, moving cities, and so forth).

The number one reason for having a personal board of directors is to put people into place to support you, encourage you, help you see potential pitfalls, and help you keep your commitments to move forward in healthy ways.

Conclusion

Now It's Time to Dream Again

You may arrive at the end of this book thinking *How is this my life? Why did I get myself into this mess? What did I miss seeing when we were dating that could have helped me avoid all this suffering? And why did I put up with so much dysfunction for so long?*

Friend, let me (Lysa) assure you: This was not your dream or your vision. The twists and turns you've gone through in your story were not part of the plan. The very fact that you are reading this book lets me know that really hard things have happened in what you thought would be a safe and loving relationship. And now you find yourself reeling from heartbreak and confusion about the death of your marriage.

Many times I've lain in bed replaying scenes from the past, wondering where it all went so wrong. So many memories. So many hopes. So many crushed dreams. So many tears.

Jim has told me time and time again, "Lysa, when you know

better, you do better." It's not going to help to berate yourself for what you didn't see, why you didn't make different choices, why you didn't get help sooner, or even what you could have done differently. So don't get caught in constant thought spirals over what you didn't know back then. And don't shame yourself for not knowing the future. None of us knew what would happen.

But let's take what we know now and determine four things.

- *We will stop trying to understand our ex-spouse and why they did the things they did.*

  I am still working on this. Partly because sometimes new hurtful things happen. I can easily find my mind spinning and saying, "I can't believe he said that or is now doing this." That's when I have to stop myself and say, "Actually, I can believe this, because it's pretty consistent with past experiences." Instead of going into an emotional tailspin, I see it for what it is and decide that if I need to respond, I will keep my boundaries and not let this chaos derail me emotionally.
- *We will work on ourselves and not them.*

  It's no longer our job to save them, fix them, or help them escape the consequences of their choices. Actually, that should have never been our job in the first place. It's now time to focus on our healing, our growth, and our future.
- *We will take the time we need to heal before jumping into another relationship.*

  It took me a long time to even envision another relationship. But I am grateful for those years, because I needed to do a lot of work inside me before I attempted another relationship. For me, the dysfunction I lived in with my first marriage had become normal. Therefore, if I didn't work to redefine what is and is not healthy in relationships, I would run the risk of being attracted to the same kinds of dysfunctions as before. I didn't want to need another man to help me heal and ease the ache of my loneliness. Yes, after experiencing so much rejection, that would have felt good temporarily, but I think I would have settled in ways I shouldn't. I wanted to be healed enough to want the right kind of man. I needed to set my future self up for success by waiting, healing, and developing healthy boundaries. The goal wasn't to find joy in another man. The goal was to be a healthy and God-honoring woman.

- *Our lives aren't over.*

  It's really hard to see this when you've imagined a future with only one person. I know it's sometimes hard to walk toward a future you don't want. But trust me, there's still a really big world out there full of new joys you don't want to miss. It's okay to still grieve over what will never be but let that be coupled with a new hope for good possibilities. Let yourself dream, imagine, discover, and pray as you walk into each new day from here.

As you close this book, please know Jim and Joel and I are praying for you. We have mentally placed you in God's faithful hands, and we trust that He will guide you, help you, encourage you, and lavish His perfect love on you. One day, I hope we get to sit down and share with each other all the good that you and I have both discovered in the process of God making beauty from ashes. That will be a really sweet day.

Care and Counseling Resources

Dear friend,

We hope this book has provided emotional fortitude and biblical confidence for the hard circumstances you may be facing right now. We also acknowledge that this is only a starting place for additional help and support. So we've put together a list of resources below that we recommend. We are praying for you and honored to be on this journey with you.

—Lysa TerKeurst, Dr. Joel Muddamalle, and Jim Cress

- Proverbs 31 Ministries: The trusted friend who wants to help you know the Truth and live the Truth because when you do, it changes everything.

  Visit www.proverbs31.org to gain access to free *Encouragement for Today* devotions, podcast episodes, biblical teachings through the First 5 app, and so much more.
- *Therapy & Theology* podcast hosted by Lysa TerKeurst

  Visit therapyandtheologypodcast.com.

- The American Association of Christian Counselors

  Visit AACC.net to find a counselor in your area by zip code.
- National Domestic Violence Hotline

  Visit thehotline.org or call 1-800-799-7233 (SAFE). The site offers anonymous help or practical next steps for those facing domestic violence or abuse.
- Counseling Intensives with Jim Cress

  If you are interested in doing a counseling intensive with Jim, visit his website at www.jimcress.com.
- Haven Place Retreats

  Visit www.havenplace.org.

Books

If you want a more extensive read on the related subjects below, check out these books.

- Learning to live loved after rejection: *Uninvited* by Lysa TerKeurst
- Disappointment and life not looking like you'd hoped: *It's Not Supposed to Be This Way* by Lysa TerKeurst
- When forgiveness feels impossible: *Forgiving What You Can't Forget* by Lysa TerKeurst
- "Is God really okay with boundaries and me saying, 'No more'?": *Good Boundaries and Goodbyes* by Lysa TerKeurst
- Moving toward healthy relationships again after broken trust: *I Want to Trust You, but I Don't* by Lysa TerKeurst
- "Why do bad things happen to humble people?": *The Hidden Peace* by Joel Muddamalle

Photo by Meshali Mitchell

You are invited to a special counseling intensive with Lysa, Jim, and Joel at Haven Place

Join us for a unique retreat designed to help you heal from emotional and relational trauma. You'll have time with Lysa, Jim, and Joel both in main teaching sessions and small-group breakout intensive work.

We limit these retreats to only fifty to sixty women, with fewer than twenty women in a small group. Plus, our time together will give you the emotional fortitude and biblical confidence to take the next steps toward moving forward in healthy ways.

If you'd like more information about attending one of our upcoming retreats, visit www.HavenPlace.org.

Notes

Chapter 1: A House Cut in Two

1. Brené Brown, *The Gifts of Imperfection* (Hazelden, 2010), 15.
2. Timothy George, *Galatians: An Exegetical and Theological Exposition of Holy Scripture*, The New American Commentary, vol. 30 (B&H Publishing Group, 1994), 418.
3. George, *Galatians*, 418.
4. "The 3 Cs of Al-Anon," Camelback Recovery, last updated October 21, 2024, https://www.camelbackrecovery.com/blog/the-3-cs-of-al-anon/.

Chapter 2: What About My Covenant with God?

1. Herman Bavinck, et al., *Reformed Dogmatics: God and Creation*, vol. 2 (Baker Academic, 2004), 555.
2. Joel Muddamalle, *The Hidden Peace: Finding True Security, Strength, and Confidence Through Humility* (Thomas Nelson, 2024), 40.
3. For a more academic reading, see Todd Scacewater, "Divorce and Remarriage in Deuteronomy 24:1–4," *Journal for the Evangelical Study of the Old Testament 1, no. 1 (2012).* For a more accessible article, see C. J. H. Wright, "Family." In *The Anchor Yale Bible Dictionary*, edited by David Noel Freedman (Doubleday, 1992).
4. J. Knox Chamblin, *Matthew: A Mentor Commentary*, Mentor Commentaries (Mentor, 2010), 924.
5. Gary Harlan Hall, *Deuteronomy*, The College Press NIV Commentary (College Press Pub. Co., 2000), 359.

6. David Instone-Brewer, *Divorce and Remarriage in the Bible: The Social and Literary Context* (William B. Eerdmans, 2002), 5–6. Brewer said, "The dowry continued to belong to the bride, so if her husband died or divorced her, she had money to live on. She might also get a portion of the estate in addition to her dowry."
7. This is not suggesting that we get a free pass to do whatever we want. There are still responsibilities that come with being in relationship with God. This statement is more about a rejection of the concept that we have to work in order to receive or earn the love of God.
8. This resource is the brilliant creation of internationally recognized trauma expert Dr. Marilyn Murray, 307.

Chapter 3: But Doesn't God Hate Divorce?

1. The KJV 1611, later updated to the New King James Version (NKJV), was forced into moving from a "translation" decision into making an "interpretation" decision to clear up the ambiguity of the original Hebrew language. This is a regular practice of all translations. However, the challenge is that the interpretive decision does not necessarily have to be the only interpretation. I want to emphasize the fact that there is good textual evidence to opt for an alternative reading that is actually more historic and predates the KJV 1611.
2. The most coherent translation that flows with ancient sources Masoretic Text (also known as MSS), Septuagint (or LXX), 4QXII, Targum, and Vulgate, (especially LXX, the first translation of the Hebrew Bible into Greek that gives us commentary level insights into the MSS) is to preserve the MSS without emendation or modification. So, we should translate it as a third-person verb "he hates." Who is the "he"? It's a reference to the husband, not God. Almost all phrases of "says Yahweh" in Malachi are taken in direct discourse, so the same should be done here—*not* indirect as KJV and NKJV opt for. So Yahweh is talking about the husband who hates and divorces his wife. The LXX supports this view and reads "allà èàn misḗsas èxapostéilēs" the construct is a participle and subjunctive (if hating you divorce or if out of hatred you divorce). This is talking about the husband, *not* God.
3. E. Lipiński, "אֱנָשׁ," ed. G. Johannes Botterweck, Helmer Ringgren, and Heinz-Josef Fabry, trans. Douglas W. Stott, *Theological Dictionary of the Old Testament* (William B. Eerdmans, 2004), 164.
4. E. Lipiński, "אֱנָשׁ," 164.
5. Brené Brown, *The Gifts of Imperfection* (Hazelden, 2010), 70.

Chapter 4: Is the Only Valid Reason for Divorce Sexual Infidelity?

1. Peter C. Craigie, "The Book of Deuteronomy," in *The New International Commentary on the Old Testament* (William B. Eerdmans, 1976), 305. The rabbinic schools of Hillel and Shammai also disagreed on this. The school of Shammai held a very conservative interpretation, believing it referred to sexual promiscuity. The school of Hillel had a very liberal view of this, where it could be anything that was displeasing, even the burning of food. For more see Todd Scacewater, "Divorce and Remarriage in Deuteronomy 24:1–4," *Journal for the Evangelical Study of the Old Testament* 1, no. 1 (2012): 67.
2. David Instone-Brewer, *Divorce and Remarriage in the Bible: The Social and Literary Context* (William B. Eerdmans, 2002), 38.
3. Instone-Brewer, *Divorce and Remarriage*, 20.
4. Instone-Brewer, *Divorce and Remarriage*, 86.
5. Robert H. Stein, "'Is It Lawful for a Man to Divorce His Wife?,'" *Journal of the Evangelical Theological Society* 22, no. 2 (1979): 117, https://etsjets.org/wp-content/uploads/2010/08/files_JETS-PDFs_22_22-2_22-2-pp115-121_JETS.pdf
6. Instone-Brewer, *Divorce and Remarriage*, 159.
7. Scott Peck, *The Road Less Traveled* (Simon & Schuster, 1978), 50.

Chapter 5: Why Hasn't God Stopped All This from Happening?

1. As a point of clarification, this is not to be taken as "God causes evil."
2. Albrecht Oepke, "Ὅπλον, Ὁπλίζω, Πανοπλία, Ζώννυμι, Διαζώννυμι, Περιζώννυμι, Ζώνη, Θώραξ, Ὑποδέω (ὑπόδημα, Σανδάλιον), Θυρεός, Περικεφαλαία," in Theological Dictionary of the New Testament, ed. Gerhard Kittel, et al., (Grand Rapids, MI: Eerdmans, 1964–), 303.
3. Lynn H. Cohick, *The Letter to the Ephesians*, ed. Ned B. Stonehouse et al., New International Commentary on the Old and New Testament (Eerdmans, 2020), 418.
4. Joel Muddamalle, *The Hidden Peace: Finding True Security, Strength, and Confidence Through Humility* (Thomas Nelson, 2024), 207.
5. Ala Yankouskaya et al., "Short-Term Head-Out Whole-Body Cold-Water Immersion Facilitates Positive Affect and Increases Interaction Between Large-Scale Brain Networks," *Biology* 12, no. 2 (2023): 211, https://doi.org/10.3390/biology12020211.
6. Yankouskaya et al., "Short-Term Head-Out Whole-Body Cold-Water Immersion."

Chapter 6: Life Changes, but You Get to Decide How You Change

1. Steven Knight, writer, *All the Light We Cannot See*, "Episode 3," directed by Shawn Levy, released November 3, 2023, Netflix.
2. I think in the categories of the classic five stages of grief outlined years ago by Dr. Elisabeth Kubler-Ross in her epic book *On Death and Dying* (MacMillan, 1969).
3. Lorie Johnson, "The Deadly Consequences of Unforgiveness," CBN, June 22, 2015, https://cbn.com/news/news/deadly-consequences-unforgiveness.

Chapter 7: It's Time to Take the High Ground You Were Meant to Occupy

1. Lysa TerKeurst, *Unglued: Making Wise Choices in the Midst of Raw Emotions* (Zondervan, 2012).
2. George H. Guthrie, "2 Corinthians," eds. Robert W. Yarbrough and Robert H. Stein, in *Baker Exegetical Commentary on the New Testament* (Baker Academic, 2015), 474. I deviate a little from Guthrie's threefold progression by talking about conformation of thoughts. Guthrie is talking about Roman military context, which is accurate and helpful.
3. George H. Guthrie, "2 Corinthians," eds. Robert W. Yarbrough and Robert H. Stein, in *Baker Exegetical Commentary on the New Testament* (Baker Academic, 2015), 474. I deviate a little from Guthrie's threefold progression by talking about conformation of thoughts. Guthrie is talking about Roman military context, which is accurate and helpful.

Chapter 8: Forgiveness Feels So Incredibly Unfair

1. This was something I learned from a tour guide on a trip studying the places where Paul did missionary journeys.
2. If you'd like more guidance on this, check out Lysa's book *Good Boundaries and Goodbyes,* where you will find an even deeper, biblical dive into boundaries. Plus, you'll find commentary from Jim throughout that book as well.